WONDERDADS

THE BEST DAD/CHILD ACTIVITIES IN INDIANAPOLIS

917.77
L58

CONTACT WONDERDADS

WonderDads books may be purchased for educational and promotional use. For information, please email us at store@wonderdads.com.

If you are interested in partnership opportunities with WonderDads, please email us at partner@wonderdads.com.

If you are interested in selling WonderDads books and other products in your region, please email us at hiring@wonderdads.com.

For corrections, recommendations on what to include in future versions of the book, updates or any other information, please email us at info@wonderdads.com.

©2011 WonderDads, Inc.

Book Authored by Angela Arlington & the WonderDads Staff.

Cover and book design by Crystal Langley. Proofread by Megan Fearon & the WonderDads Staff.

All rights reserved. Printed in the United States of America.

ISBN: 978-1-935153-58-0
First Printing, 2011
10 9 8 7 6 5 4 3 2 1

WONDERDADS
INDIANAPOLIS
Table of Contents

WELCOME TO WONDERDADS INDIANAPOLIS

Like so many other Dads, I love being with my kids, but struggle to find the right work/home balance. We are a part of a generation where Dads play much more of an active role with their kids, yet the professional and financial strains are greater than ever. We hope that the ideas in this book make it a little easier to be inspired to do something that makes you a hero in the eyes of your children.

This part of our children's lives goes by too fast, but the memories from a WonderDads inspired trip, event, meal, or activity last a long time (and will probably be laughed about when they grow up). So plan a Daddy day once a week, make breakfast together every Saturday morning, watch your football team every Sunday, or whatever works for you, and be amazed how long they will remember the memories and how good you will feel about yourself in the process.

Our warmest welcome to WonderDads.

Sincerely,

Jonathan Aspatore, **Founder & Dad**
Charlie (4) and Luke (3)

TOP 10 OVERALL BEST DAD/CHILD THINGS TO DO:

THE BEST OF INDIANAPOLIS

THE TOP 5 DAD/CHILD RESTAURANTS

THE TOP 5 DAD/CHILD ACTIVITIES

THE TOP 5 DAD/CHILD OUTDOOR PARKS AND RECREATION

THE TOP 5 DAD/CHILD THINGS TO DO ON A SUNNY DAY

THE TOP 5 DAD/CHILD FULL-DAY ACTIVITIES

THE TOP 5 DAD/CHILD SPLURGES $$$

THE TOP 5 DAD/CHILD MOST MEMORABLE

THE BEST DAD/CHILD
RESTAURANTS

APPLEBEE'S
Broad Ripple

1072 Broad Ripple Ave.
Indianapolis, IN 46220
(317) 255-4839

This Broad Ripple restaurant is within walking distance of the high school. They have a great kids' menu and dad can eat half-price appetizers from 4pm-6pm on Monday-Thursday. Kids menu comes with crayons to color on the paper menu and amuse the kids while waiting for their food. The French fries are lightly seasoned so they do not taste bland at all. Kids and dads can order dessert shots in different flavors. They are a great sized dessert perfect for everyone.

BISCUITS CAFÉ
Broad Ripple

1035 Broad Ripple Ave.
Indianapolis, IN 46220
(317) 202-0410

Dads and kids will enjoy eating at this Broad Ripple café. Dads in the area rave about the special gravy used on the biscuits. This is a great place to eat after strolling through the middle of Broad Ripple on the main street.

BOOGIE BURGER
Broad Ripple

927 E Westfield Blvd.
Indianapolis, IN 46220
(317) 255-2450

This has a small burger counter with patio seating in the middle of Broad Ripple. Dads will want to order the giant third-of-a- pound burger loaded with toppings. The kids will not be able to eat such a huge burger, but they will love eating huge bags of fries topped with garlic and parsley.

GOOD MORNING MAMA'S CAFE
Broad Ripple

1001 E 54th St.
Indianapolis, IN 46220
(317) 255-3800 | www.goodmorningmamas.com

This café is located in what once was an old gas station in Broad Ripple. Dads and kids that like brunch should try eating here—you can even sit outside and eat if you want on sunny mornings. The menu selections for both breakfast and lunch are creative and full of variety. Some of the items on the menu are pancakes and eggs, Loco Moco, Elvis' favorite, Eggs in Purgatory, and Italian Fried Biscuits. The Italian Fried Biscuits come 4 to an order and your kids will love them. You may need to place an extra order or two to take home with you!

3 SISTERS CAFÉ
Broad Ripple

6360 Guilford Ave.
Indianapolis, IN 46220
(317) 257-5556

Dads and kids will love this menu- many are Vegan delights. Enjoy outdoor dining for breakfast and lunch in warm months and a relaxing and quaint indoor dining experience, featuring local art and nice folk tunes through the speakers. Breakfast and lunch served daily and dinner is served on Thursday-Saturday.

BUB'S BURGERS AND ICE CREAM
Carmel

210 W Main St.
Carmel, IN 46032
(317) 706-2827

Kids get a busy bag with their meal containing crackers and a treat- all for less than $5. Dad can also find plenty to eat without spending a lot of money.

MAX AND ERMA'S
Carmel

12195 N Meridian St.
Carmel, IN 46032
(317) 705-9788

Kids eat free on Tuesdays. Dad should order an appetizer, as the best thing on the menu is cheese skewers served with a great marinara sauce for dipping each bite on the little sticks. When the kids finish their food they get to make a trash sundae from toppings like syrup, nuts, whipped cream, crushed candy and other edible stuff.

MOE'S SOUTHWEST GRILL
Carmel

12483 N Meridian St.
Carmel, IN 46032
(317) 848-6637

Kids eat free on Sundays. Moe's is a popular place for dads and kids to go to on a regular basis. The food is good and the prices are just as good for dads looking to eat out on a budget. Dads and kids will enjoy the free chips and salsa that come with every order. Mini Moe's menu has a variety of items for kids to eat, like Power Wagon, Moo Moo Mr. Cow, Mini Masterpiece, and Take Your Pik – Meals come with a beverage and cookie.

RESTAURANTS

15

RED ROBIN GOURMET BURGERS

Carmel

14599 Clay Terrace Blvd.
Carmel, IN 46032
(317) 574-0102

The gourmet burgers come in so many different ways, dad and his kids are sure to find a perfect match for their taste buds. Dads enjoy the burgers as much as the kids do here. The service is great and they are very customer oriented. Red Robin! YUMMM!

ZACKY'S HOT DOGS

Carmel

1315 S Range Line Rd.
Carmel, IN 46032
(317) 848-5088 | www.zackyshotdogs.com

People rave about the service and the wonderful hot dogs served here. Dads and kids will find a large selection of what comes on top of their hot dogs. The favorite hot dogs on the menu are named after fabulous cities – New York, Chicago, and Cincinnati. The New Yorker is a hot dog with sauerkraut and spicy brown mustard. The Chicago dog is topped with relish, pickle spears, sliced tomato, mustard, hot peppers and diced onions. The Cincinnati Dog is topped with Cincinnati chili, onions, and cheese.

JOHNNY'S ROCKETS

Downtown

Circle Center
49 W Maryland St.
Indianapolis, IN 46204
(317) 238-0444

Famous for juicy hamburgers and hand dipped shakes, there's something for everyone to enjoy. Reflect back upon 1950 with dancing servers and tabletop jukeboxes that play music for a nickel. The kids will want to play several songs, so be prepared for a noisy lunch.

MUG-N-BUN DRIVE-IN

Downtown

5211 W 10th St.
Indianapolis, IN 46224
(317) 244-5669 | www.mug-n-bun.com

A traditional 1950's drive – in that will intrigue young children who have never been served curbside. Make sure to order their root beer as it is homemade and super yummy!! Local and first time customers rave about the tenderloin sandwiches, foot long hot dogs, onion rings, fried mushrooms, and the homemade pizza. They only accept cash, so be sure to have some on you!

RAM
Downtown

140 S Illinois St.
Indianapolis, IN 46204
(317) 955-9900 | www.theram.com

Kids eat for $1 on Sundays. Many dads enjoy eating here with their families because the staff makes the meal a great experience. On the menu one of the great appetizers is fried pickles. Kids 12 and under can order kid combos. Each one comes with a veggie appetizer, side dish, a beverage, and a scoop of ice cream for dessert. Their pizza dough is made fresh daily in small batches with Big Horn Hefeweizen beer. They have many yummy combinations of burgers to choose from and the sides are great- House Fries, Ram Chips, Fireside Beans, coleslaw, or substitute: sweet potato fries, waffle fries, thick – cut Onion Rings or garlic fries $.49 each.

SCOTTY'S BREWHOUSE
Downtown

1 Virginia Ave.
Indianapolis, IN 46204
(317) 571-0808

Dads and kids will both enjoy the food here. 12 and under eat free with paid adult entrée on Tuesdays and Sundays. They offer a couple of gluten – free food items on their menu and what a huge menu it is to read! The kids will find a favorite item on the kids' menu. Two options that are not typically found on any kids' menu is Lizzie's Noodles — butter on noodles (nothing more, nothing less) and (grilled) Chicken on a Stick. The waitresses and waiters are patient and make this place a great one to come back to again.

THE OLD SPAGHETTI FACTORY
Downtown

210 S. Meridian St.
Indianapolis, IN 46225
(317) 635-6325

Dads must arrive early to beat the lunch crowd if they want to sit in a real trolley car in the middle of the restaurant, which is where all the kids want to sit. Great food for the money, recommendations for WonderDad and kids is the fettuccini Alfredo or their spaghetti with any of the sauces. You get a bowl of ice cream if your order a meal, either pistachio or Neapolitan.

17

CR HEROES FAMILY PUB
Fishers

10570 E 96th St.
Fishers, IN 46037
(317) 576-1070

Monday and Tuesday kids under 12 eat free with paid adult entrée. Face painting and balloon animals are created as your kids eat. This is a real family friendly place to eat at. Dads who eat here a lot suggest getting the ribs—they are the best in town!

FIVE GUYS FAMOUS BURGERS AND FRIES
Fishers

11670 Commercial Dr.
Fishers, IN 46038
(317) 596-8686 | www.fiveguys.com

WonderDads and kids will find large portions of food and friendly service at this restaurant. The burgers are good here, but it's the French fries that really stand apart from other places. Dad should order a small, because the large fries are around 3 huge helpings and enough to feed 3-4 people.

KING CHEF CHINESE
Fishers

8664 E 96th St.
Fishers, IN 46037
(317) 842-8989 | www.kingchefind.com

If you are looking for great Chinese food for small budgets, then you have hit the jackpot with this restaurant. Local dads and kids really like the egg rolls and egg drop soup. The crab Rangoon is a big hit for dads, but there are plenty of entrées to eat here if you don't like crab.

MCALISTER'S DELI
Fishers

8355 116th St.
Fishers, IN 46038
(317) 842-9400

Kids 12 and under eat free on Mondays with a paid adult entrée. This place is best known for their sweet tea and huge baked potatoes. The parking lot is always busy, but this is a great place to eat, so be prepared that seating might take longer than usual.

SCOTTY'S LAKEHOUSE
Fishers

10158 Brooks School Rd.
Fishers, IN 46037
(317) 577-2900

Kids eat free Monday and Saturday 8am-4pm. Some of the great food items offered here are organic meats, elk, and bison. The French fried vanilla sweet potatoes are a favorite among regular customers.

DENNY'S
Indy E

2490 Post Rd.
Indianapolis, IN 46229
(317) 899-5198

Kids 10 and under eat free on Tuesdays from 4pm-10pm. They are open 24 – hours – a – day with breakfast available all hours. They have a decent lunch and dinner menu, but the breakfast items will be what dad and his kids will want to eat. Denny's is well known for their Grand Slam Breakfast deals. No one will leave hungry after eating the Big Grand Slam.

GOLDEN CORRAL RESTAURANTS
Indy E

10220 E Washington St.
Indianapolis, IN 46229
(317) 890-0270

Kids 4 and younger are free all day at this amazing buffet restaurant. They offer salads, main entrées, side dishes, and a huge variety of desserts. The potato bar and taco bar will let the kids create their own baked potato with various toppings and tacos the way they like them.

LONESTAR STEAKHOUSE
Indy E

100087 E Washington St.
Indianapolis, IN 46229
(317) 899-3780

Kids eat free all day Tuesdays. Steak is the biggest deal at this restaurant, but they offer other foods as well, like chicken.

LONGHORN STEAKHOUSE
Indy E

10240 E Washington St.
Indianapolis, IN 46229
(317) 890-0300 | www.longhornsteakhouse.com

For Wonderdads who need a filling dinner, this place serves entrées under $25 with good portion sizes. The kids' menu here features all the favorites; grilled cheese, cheeseburger, hot dog, chicken tenders, macaroni and cheese, and 2 different items: grilled chicken salad and kids' sirloin. All Kids' Meals are served with fresh fruit, a drink and seasoned french fries (unless side is already specified). Kids' Grilled Chicken Salad is served with fresh fruit and a drink

SKYLINE CHILI
Indy E

7757 E Washington St.
Indianapolis, IN 46219
(317) 352-1275

Kids under 12 eat for $.99 on Fridays from 5pm-9pm. You can get your chili plain or topped with a variety of toppings like cheese, onions, and sauce. Some dads think the chili here is the best in the area.

19

A 2 Z ITALIAN CAFÉ   Indy N

4705 East 96th St.
Indianapolis, IN 46240
(317) 569-9349

Kids eat free on Wednesdays at this great café. Anything dad orders here will be yummy, but the spaghetti is a surefire hit every day.

BIG MIKE'S CAFE AMERICANA   Indy N

9611 College Ave.
Indianapolis, IN 46280
(317) 571-1000

This is a great place to find Italian cooking at its best with huge portions of food. Wonderdad and his kids can't go wrong with ordering the flavorful burgers, baked tortellini, stuffed chicken, or the BEST lasagna in the area. It is made to order and has big chunks of mushrooms, tomatoes, ground beef, and pepperoni in it. It costs less than $10 and comes with a yummy garlic knot roll. For lunch they serve a pizza buffet that the kids might enjoy more than the menu items listed.

HOLLYHOCK HILL
FAMILY STYLE DINNING   Indy N

8110 N College Ave.
Indianapolis, IN 46240
(317) 251-2294 | www.hollyhockhill.com

This restaurant is well known for its fried chicken. Bring your hungry kids here for dinner and there will be more than enough food to fill their bellies. Be sure to call ahead to make reservations for dinner.

HOT CAKES EMPORIUM   Indy N

8555 Ditch Rd.
Indianapolis, IN 46260
(317) 254-5993

Your kids will be speechless as they stuff their mouths full of pancakes at this restaurant that is a hit with the neighborhood. Open for breakfast and lunch only.

PUCCINI'S   Indy N

1508 W 86th St.
Indianapolis, IN 46260
(317) 875-9223

Dads and kids love the food here and the price is great for pizza or pasta dishes. Ask for whatever you want on your pizza- clams on top are a favorite of some customers. Going at lunch time can get you a meal with salad and pasta or small pizza with a salad- enough food to fill your tummy.

BENNIGAN'S IRISH AMERICAN GRILL AND TAVERN

Indy NE

7701 E 42nd St.
Indianapolis, IN 46226
(317) 613-2366

Tuesdays from 4pm-10pm kids eat free. WonderDads and kids will love this restaurant for its Irish theme and tasty menu/

BUCA DI BEPPO

Indy NE

6045 E 86th St.
Indianapolis, IN 46250
(317) 842-8666 | www.bucadibeppo.com

Dads and kids will need an empty stomach before they come here to eat all the yummy food. This restrauant serves family–style food in two portion sizes; Buca Small® feeds up to three people and Buca Large® feeds an average of six people.

CHICK-FIL-A

Indy NE

3802 E 82nd St.
Indianapolis, IN 46250
(317) 578-4511

Children 12 and under eat free with paid adult entrée on Wednesdays from 4pm-8pm. The restaurant is located near the Castleton Square Mall, so dads can come here after shopping or watching a movie at the AMC Theater down the road with his kids. This is a great fast food place that is not greasy or full of cholesterol. As the cows like to say, "Eat More Chicken!!"

HOULIHAN'S

Indy NE

Located in Castleton Square Mall
6020 E 82nd St.
Indianapolis, IN 46250
(317) 845-9428 | www.houlihans.com

This is a family friendly restaurant that offers dads entrées for $15 or less. The menu features American favorites, gluten–free items and a good kids' menu. Families that eat here often remark on the great atmosphere and how friendly the service is. Recommendations for here are to try the pickle fries and the flatbread pizza.

21

THE MELTING POT
Indy NE

5650 E 86th St.
Indianapolis, IN 46250
(317) 841-3601 | www.meltingpot.com

This is one of Indianapolis' Most Romantic Date Places, but Wonderdad will love it just eating with his kids. Here it is okay to double dip your food. There is a great variety of cheeses to choose from for dipping—bread, meat, chicken, whatever dad orders to go with the cheese fondue pot. For dessert the chocolate fondue is delicious and is great for dipping fruits and other sweet treats into.

ABUELO'S
Indy NW

5910 W 86th St
Indianapolis, IN 46278
(317) 876-0250 | www.abuelos.com

This restaurant is near several great stores on busy 86th St. Dads and kids should try the Abuelo's dip sampler, which is a popular choice for regular customers. Some of the dishes they have are salmon Santa Cruz, Alambre De Camaron, some gluten–free food, Vegan dishes, and a nice kids' menu.

BRAVO!
Indy NW

2658 Lake Circle Dr.
Indianapolis, IN 46268
(317) 879-1444 | www.bravoitalian.com

This is a little bit more expensive than many of the other restaurants listed, but the food is worth every penny. They open daily at 11am, but on Sundays they serve only brunch from 11am-3pm. Dads and kids can see the staff working at the ovens and cooking pizzas while they wait for their food. Bread comes warm and crispy to dip into an olive oil mix. Most of the items are good, but one recommendation is to order the Cheese Ravioli Al Forno, listed as an appetizer. It could be a meal all on its own and it comes out looking beautiful on the plate.

CICI'S PIZZA
Indy NW

3459 W 86th St.
Indianapolis, IN 46268
(317) 471-8001

Pizza lovers will be delighted by the buffet. A variety of pizzas, garlic bread, salad bar, and deserts are included. Wonderdads should encourage the kids to try the delicious Alfredo Pizza or the Spinach Alfredo pizza to get some veggies in the meal.

KAZAN JAPANESE STEAKHOUSE   Indy NW

2412 Lake Circle Dr.
Indianapolis, IN 46268
(317) 337-2000

Kids will think you have super powers after watching the chef cook their meal in front of them. Lots of dicing, throwing things up in the air, and fire add magic to this dining experience. The fried rice is good with anything dad orders—beef, fish, or plain vegetables.

LE PEEP RESTAURANT   Indy NW

6335 Intech Commons Dr.
Indianapolis, IN 46278
(317) 298-7337 | www.lepeepindy.com

This little restaurant is open every day for breakfast and lunch hours only. Dads and kids who like to eat brunch will be pleased with the menu. The omelets are good, as well as the yogurt parfait they serve with a piece of toast or an English muffin. They have a good kids' menu—they might want to try the French toast with lots of syrup. Everything on the menu is less than $10 per entrée, so dad can feel good about saving money while enjoying great food.

BUFFALO WILD WINGS   Indy W

6135 W 25th St.
Indianapolis, IN 46224
(317) 241-9464 | www.buffalowildwings.com

Chicken lovers will love eating wings here. There are 14 different sauces to try on your wings. WonderDad may be brave enough to try the hottest type, but most of the kids will probably stick with the honey barbeque or other mild flavors.

GRINDSTONE CHARLEY'S   Indy W

5822 Crawfordsville Rd.
Indianapolis, IN 46234
(317) 481-1870

Kids eat free on Wednesdays. Let your kids be wowed by a magician creating balloon creatures and doing magic tricks. The kids' menu is good and WonderDad will find burgers, chicken, and other favorites to eat here.

PARAGON FAMILY RESTAURANT

Indy W

118 S Girls School Rd.
Indianapolis, IN 46231
(317) 271-3514 | www.paragonrestaurant.biz

Many families come here at least once a week and its all due to the owner and the great food. This is a popular restaurant for the after-church crowd: large portions, tons of specials (most places have one or two on a sign. Paragon has a white board crammed with selections). Anything that sounds like a good home-cooked meal is a safe bet: fried chicken, meat loaf, even liver and onions. The menu is huge, so WonderDad and his kids will enjoy eating here. They offer a free dessert night on Fridays.

SONIC DRIVE-IN

Indy W

66 S Raceway Rd.
Indianapolis, IN 46231
(317) 272-4379

This is a great place for milkshakes and hotdogs without having to leave your car. The kids will think it is cool when the waitress brings the tray to your car. This is a lovely place to eat when it's spring or fall because the kids can enjoy a warm breeze as they eat with the car windows down. WonderDad will like the prices on the menu as all the items are inexpensive and taste great.

3 IN 1 RESTAURANT

Indy W

4810 W 34th St.
Indianapolis, IN 46224
(317) 543-7770 | www.3in1restaurant.com

The three types of food dads and kids will find here are Mexican, Barbeque, and Latin American. This restaurant has done a great job of combining these three cultural types into their own one-of-a-kind flavor. Some suggestions to try are the sweet corn tamales and the pupusas.

CARRABBA'S ITALIAN GRILL

Southport

4690 Southport Crossings Dr.
Southport, IN 46237
(317) 881-4008

From the wood-fire grilled chicken to the mouthwatering steaks, many customers rate this restaurant with 5 stars. Dads will pour over the menu and no matter what he orders it will be good. The kids can choose food off the Bambini Menu. Drinks are included with 5 available choices: grilled chicken breast, spaghetti with meatballs, cheese or pepperoni pizza, cheese ravioli with tomato sauce, and, the traditional favorite, chicken fingers. The staff is very cordial and willing to meet the customers' needs.

CHEESEBURGER IN PARADISE
Southport

4670 Southport Crossings Dr
Indianapolis, IN 46237
(317) 883-4386

This place is modeled after Jimmy Buffet. WonderDad will love the food here and the kids' meals are yummy. The kids' menu includes mini–cheeseburgers, cheese quesadilla, chicken quesadilla, corn dogs, chicken fingers, Captain Mac 'n Cheese, and grilled chicken breast. All kids receive a complimentary snow cone.

RUBY TUESDAY
Southport

7940 US 31 S
Indianapolis, IN 46227
(317) 885-5801 | www.rubytuesday.com

WonderDads love the ribs served here and have recommended that everyone try them. The Salad Bar is a meal all by itself. There is such a huge variety of foods to eat here. Visit the Endless Fresh Garden Bar and make your very own salad sensation. The bar has fresh garden greens, crisp vegetables, premium cheeses and toppings, and a variety of dressings. All meals come with made–from–scratch Garlic Cheese Biscuits—they are really good. The kids' menu offers pasta, mini–burgers, the fresh salad bar, chicken strips, grilled chicken, fried shrimp, and chop steak.

RYAN'S
Southport

8180 US 31 S
Indianapolis, IN 46227
(317) 881-1156

WonderDad is in the mood for fried chicken, but his kid wants shrimp. No debating, this is the place to go to. Kids 3 and younger free all day at the great American buffet. Try the breaded corn nuggets or the freshly made rolls. Both are delicious!

TEDDY'S BURGER JOINT
Southport

2222 W Southport Rd Suite B
Indianapolis, IN 46217
(317) 893-2791 | www.teddysburgerjoint.com

They have a variety of items to try on their menu. WonderDads might want to try a bison burger Cajun Style or a Teddy Bear Burger. They offer many different types of mayo; try tasting it by asking for it on the side. The place is set up like a picnicking area. Picnic tables with paper towels as napkins are set up along with regular tables for those who are less messy when they eat. The kids will have a super fantastic time when they see the playroom. It is set up with a huge sandbox and the kids can even draw on the floor!

25

THE BEST DAD/CHILD
ACTIVITIES

BROAD RIPPLE ART FESTIVAL   Broad Ripple

820 E 67th St.
Indianapolis, IN 46220
(317) 255-2464

This festival is held in May every year and brings more than 225 artists to one place. There is a great kids' area with activities and live music and entertainment on stage through out the 2-day event.

BROAD RIPPLE FARMERS MARKET   Broad Ripple

Broad Ripple Ave.
Indianapolis, IN 46220
(317) 251-2782 | broadripplefarmersmarket@gmail.com

Open during Memorial Day until Labor Day, this is a great place to find food produced by local farmers. Dad and kids will enjoy seeing all the fruit, vegetables, handmade products, and other treats from different vendors.

BROAD RIPPLE PARK RECREATION CENTER   Broad Ripple

1550 Broad Ripple Ave.
Indianapolis, IN 46220
(317) 327-7161 | www.indyparks.com

This is a special event that takes place after Thanksgiving. Dad and his kids will love making a gingerbread house together at this annual event. Call for more information ahead of time.

GLENDALE BRANCH LIBRARY   Broad Ripple

6101 N Keystone Ave.
Indianapolis, IN 46220
(317) 275- 4410

Baby story time is on Tuesdays at 10:30am. The Paws to Read Program is available for 6-11 year olds, but WonderDad must call to register for 10 minute sessions of reading with the dog. This library is located inside of the Glendale Mall.

INDIANAPOLIS ART CENTER   Broad Ripple

820 E 67th St.
Indianapolis, IN 46220
(317) 255-2464 | www.indplsartcenter.org

Dads and kids will love this center filled with local artwork and different rotating exhibits throughout the year. Eight exhibit rooms are filled with original artworks. They offer art classes for kids and dads in a variety of mediums—painting, sculpting, glass blowing, and drawing to name a few courses. Admission is always free, donations are appreciated.

KILN CREATIONS
Broad Ripple

918 Broad Ripple Ave.
Indianapolis, IN 46220
(317) 251-2386 | www.kilncreations.biz

Little ones and WonderDad can be creative all they want and make secret gifts for others around birthdays and the holidays.

RED MANGO
Broad Ripple

914 Broad Ripple Ave.
Indianapolis, IN 46220
(317) 259-5000

Anyone in the house who is on a gluten–free diet will love finding yummy yogurt in Broad Ripple. Available in many flavors with added pro–biotic, this is a treat well deserved for walking along the village.

ROCKY RIPPLE ART FESTIVAL
Broad Ripple

842 W 53rd St.
Indianapolis, IN 46220
www.rockyripple.org

In October this festival is free and fun for all ages. WonderDad and his kids will love looking at local artists and interactive children's services.

BOUNCER TOWN
Carmel

14455 Clay Terrace Blvd.
Carmel, IN 46032
(317) 571-8696 | www.bouncertown.com

Open play every day of the week—no reservations required. Kids will love the giant inflatable climbing structures, arcade, interactive games, and the chance to win prizes and toys.

CARMEL CYCLERY
Carmel

260 W Carmel Dr.
Carmel, IN 46032
(317) 575-8588

Enjoy a rental bicycle ride throughout the heart of Carmel all the way to Broad Ripple. Pedal the paved Monon Greenway or create your own route (map.google.com/biking) on a comfortable bicycle or tandem. Free locks, helmets, and trail maps. This is a great way for dads and kids to get around, as the Monon trail starts in Indianapolis and continues through Westfield right now.

CARMEL FEST
Carmel

Carmel, IN 46032

(317) 581-0331 | www.carmelfest.net

One of the best activities to do on July 4th! Live music and entertainment on stage, food vendors, and crafts for sale make this festival a busy event. The huge parade that travels down 126th St. and on to Range Line Rd. consists of marching bands, clowns, church floats, local companies' floats, the mayor, the marines, and dancing girls. Bring a bag to carry the candy collected by the kids from the participants in the parade. There are fireworks at dusk both nights.

CARMEL ICE STADIUM
Carmel

1040 3rd Ave. SW

Carmel, IN 46032

(317) 844-8884

When your kids want to ice skate you can go, even in the summer. Open year round and offers skate rental and a snack bar.

CARMEL PUBLIC LIBRARY
Carmel

55 4th Ave SE

Carmel, IN 46032

(317) 844-3363 | www.carmel.lib.in.us

Baby story time is on Thursdays at 10am, 11am, and 12pm. Call the Children's and Youth Services for more information on other activities. Many activities for families also take place throughout the year. This is one of the biggest libraries in the area and the children's section offers more than just books. There are computers to play on, a section with little kids toys to entertain toddlers, and an enjoyable experience for kids and dads.

LASER FLASH
Carmel

617 3rd Ave. SW

Carmel, IN 46032

(317) 571-1677 | www.laser-flash.com

This is a great fun place to play laser tag and redemption games. They also have good pizza and snacks to order for hungry bodies. WonderDads and kids can play, but the computer decides who is on the green or red teams. Many kids have birthday parties here, so WonderDad should ask about party packages as the kids play.

MONON AQUATIC CENTER
Carmel

1235 Central Park Dr. W

Carmel, IN, 46032

(317) 848-7275

Open daily from Memorial Day to Labor Day. This center has an outdoor pool with water play structures, a diving pool, two water slides, a lazy river (with two rainfalls along the way,) a sand box area and a water play area for WonderDads and their kids 5 and under.

REGAL VILLAGE PARK STADIUM
Carmel

2222 E 146th St.
Carmel, IN 46033
(317) 843-1666

Movies before 12pm are $5 for everyone. In the summertime they have free family movies on Tuesday and Wednesday mornings. Smaller sized then newer theaters, the theater has a more cozy and familiar atmosphere for families who come often.

THE MUSEUM OF MINIATURE HOUSES
Carmel

111 E Main St.
Carmel, IN 46032
(317) 575-9466

WonderDads with little girls who love dolls will have to visit here. Along with the displayed miniature exhibits, the museum has a gift shop with a selection of unusual miniatures, books, and periodicals all about miniatures and dollhouses. A museum Treasure Hunt Game is provided for children of all ages to extend the fun.

THE PERFORMING ARTS CENTER
Carmel

355 City Center Dr.
Carmel, IN 46032
(317) 843-3800

Home of The Tarkington, The Studio Theater, and the impressive Palladium, this is Carmel's new place for performing arts. This center was created to bring more performing art groups to Carmel. Dads and kids alike will be impressed by all the detailed work put into these three sections of the center.

CENTRAL LIBRARY
Downtown

40 E Clair St.
Indianapolis, IN 46204
(317) 275-4100

The Children's area in this library holds over 2.1 million books, movies, CDs, and other stuff that kids love. Little kids will want to go to the Learning Curve, where they can hear lots of stories aloud. In the Make Believe Theater, kids can dress up and act out stories in front of a rotated background linked to be viewed on television nearby. There are plenty of cozy book nooks to nestle into.

CHOCOLATE CAFÉ THE SOUTH BEND CHOCOLATE COMPANY

Downtown

20 N Meridian St.
Indianapolis, IN 46204
(317) 951-4816

Walk around the famous Indianapolis Monument Circle during the cold night skies of December to see the bright lights decorating Soldiers and Sailors Monument. The inside of the Monument is open Wednesday-Sunday from 10:30am-5:30pm. Inside the monument, kids can walk the 333 steps to the top or take the elevator. The Colonel Eli Lilly Civil War Museum is located on the lower level and has a collection of Civil War exhibits and Artifacts. Afterwards, treat yourself and your kids to hot chocolate and other yummy treats to warm you from your toes to your nose at the Chocolate Café.

CITY-COUNTY BUILDING

Downtown

200 E Washington St.
Indianapolis, IN 46204
(317) 236-4345

This is a free activity for dads and kids to enjoy. Go up to the 28th floor to see Indianapolis from this height. Exhibits and scale models of different places are also part of the adventure.

EITELJORG MUSEUM OF AMERICAN INDIANS AND WESTERN ART

Downtown

500 W Washington St.
Indianapolis, IN 46204
(317) 636-9378 | www.eiteljorg.org

Visit Discovery Junction for hands-on activities. Staff members come alive as they do crafts or tell stories to young children. This museum immerses visitors into the culture of the American West and Native America. Every Saturday at 12:30pm there is a Native-American Drum Circle. The first Tuesday of every month is discount day.

GREATIMES FUN PARK   Downtown

5341 Elmwood Ave.
Indianapolis, IN 46203
(317) 780-0300

This indoor, climate – controlled, multi – level fun park will be a hit with the kids. It has bumper boats, arcades, go – karts, batting cages, miniature golf, food services, and over 5,000 feet of play area set aside for climbers, runners, sliders and all.

INDIANAPOLIS MOTOR SPEEDWAY
HALL OF FAME MUSEUM   Downtown

4790 W 16th St.
Indianapolis, IN 46222
(317) 484-6747 | www.indy500.com

Faster then a speeding bullet, here comes WonderDad racing to see over 75 racing, classic, and antique cars in person. Then thrill the kids with a ride on the minibus tour around the racetrack.

INDIANAPOLIS ZOO   Downtown

1200 W Washington St.
Indianapolis, IN 46222
(317) 630-2001 | www.indyzoo.com

Come see the dolphins in the amazing aquarium underwater, or watch them from above as they do flips during daily dolphin shows. Different sections of the zoo include biomes for snakes, birds, desert animals, and all the animals you expect to see. The polar bear is quite popular as he sits on his island or if you visit down below he'll swim right past you—your kids will feel like he touched them through the glass. The first Tuesday of every month is discount day.

INDIANA STATE MUSEUM   Downtown

650 W Washington St.
Indianapolis, IN 46204
(800) 665-9065. 232-1637

Three floors of permanent and special exhibits can be found here ranging from the birth of Earth to the 21st Century. WonderDad can show his kids Indiana history in a way they haven't seen it before. Also see a movie in 3D at the IMAX Theater and get a big kick out of any movie that's showing. The museum is always closed on Mondays but the first Tuesday of every month is discount day.

INDY TILT STUDIOS
FAMILY FUN CENTER   Downtown

49 W Maryland St. Suite 206
Indianapolis, IN 46204
(317) 226-9267

Shopping at the Circle Center Malls can be boring for young kids. Rescue them by going to the fourth floor to discover all kinds of video games and interactive play.

IPS CRISPUS ATTUCKS MUSEUM   Downtown

1140 Dr. Martin Luther King Jr. St.
Indianapolis, IN 46202
(317) 226-2432

This museum features exciting and proactive history exhibits focusing on the African–American Experience. There are 4 galleries with 60 exhibits that celebrate historic events and the outstanding contributions made by Africans and African Americans. Open Monday–Friday from 9am-5pm and on Saturdays from 12pm-5pm.

JILLIAN'S   Downtown

141 S Meridian St.
Indianapolis, IN 46225
(317) 822-9300

Three levels of food and fun for everyone. The Amazing Game Room will keep you and your kids busy for hours. There is also food available that tastes great.

NCAA HALL OF CHAMPIONS   Downtown

700 W Washington St.
Indianapolis, IN 46204
(317) 916-4255

Sport loving dads will want to bring kids here to see the wonders of the NCAA. Galleries are filled with interactive exhibits and the history of the players will inspire little ones to play. The first Tuesday of every month is discount day.

PEEWINKLES PUPPET STUDIO   Downtown

25 E Henry St.
Indianapolis, IN 46225
(317) 283-7144 | www.peewinklespuppets.com

Puppets seen here will mesmerize both you and your kids. Every detail of the characters will amaze you as you watch while eating a bag of kid size popcorn.

34

PUBLIC TOURS OF LUCAS OIL STADIUM
Downtown

500 S Capitol Ave.
Indianapolis, IN 46225
(317) 262-8600 | www.lucasoilstadium.com/Tour/

WonderDad and his kids can tour Lucas Oil Stadium, which is where the Indianapolis Colts football team plays!

RHYTHM! DISCOVERY CENTER
Downtown

110 W Washington St. Suite A
Indianapolis, IN 46204
(317) 275-9030

Musical dads and kids will love coming to this center to explore. Interactive exhibits and hands-on activities explore rhythm with a variety of drums and percussion instruments. History and cultural connections of rhythm are shown though rare percussion instruments and artifacts from around the world.

BEN & ARI'S
Fishers

13875 Trade Center Dr.
Fishers, IN 46038
(317) 770-5294 | www.benandari.com

Unpredictable weather is no problem for WonderDad. Outside is a miniature golf course for the warm days. Inside are redemption games, interactive games and duckpin bowling to play. This is a popular place for both birthday parties and for fundraisers for local organizations. They are closed on Mondays, but open the rest of the week for lots of fun for dads and kids.

BOUNCE U
Fishers

9715 Kincaid Dr. Suite 800
Fishers, IN 46038
(317) 575-7529

WonderDad can bounce along with his kids at this party place. Open Monday-Friday 10am to 7pm, Saturday & Sunday 9am to 9pm (half-price, 1/2-hour dedicated session announced weekly, please call for specific times).

CONNOR PRAIRIE
Fishers

13400 Allisonville Rd.
Fishers, IN 46038
(317) 776-6006 | www.connorprairie.com

Amaze your kids by visiting the one of the largest living history museum in Indiana. Open daily from April to October. Visit trading posts, log cabins, Native Americans, frontiers, and the great balloon voyage. There is a trolley to drop you off at various points, but be prepared to walk a lot. This is a huge place and many times there are schools visiting and it can be crowded, so dad should call ahead if big crowds bother him or his kids. Take advantage of all the seasonal programs going on from November to March. This is the place to go on Haunted Hayrides with young kids, and tour the many incredible looking gingerbread houses entered each year for top prizes.

DIPPIN' DOTS ICE CREAM
Fishers

11760 Olio Rd. Suite 500
Fishers, IN 46037
(317) 288-0367

Dippin' Dots are the easiest way to eat ice cream with no messy hands or faces to clean up! With over 30 flavors, WonderDad can find something for everyone here. Offers ice cream, Dot Quakes, yogurt, fat-free sugar-free ice creams, sherbets, ice cream sandwiches, ice cream cake, and Frappes. One of these is sure to please everyone. Great to take along to one of the area's parks to eat and enjoy a warm day.

FISHERS FREEDOM FESTIVAL
Fishers

8601 E 116th St.
Fishers, IN 46038
(317) 595-3195

Major festival held every year the last weekend in June. Look for arts and crafts being sold, a kids' tent with activities, a teen tent with older activities, and great festival food. Admission is a donation of a non-perishable food item. Two days of great fun also include a kids-only parade and fireworks at night. Free shuttle at local churches helps dads to find parking.

FISHERS RENAISSANCE FAIRE
Fishers

13400 Allisonville Rd.
Fishers, IN 46038
www.fishersrenfaire.com

Held in October every year on the grounds of Conner Prairie, this event brings 2 full days of over 100 performances and full-contact jousting. WonderDad and his kids will love traveling back in time at this fair.

FISHERS TRAIN STATION
Fishers

11601 Municipal Dr.
Fishers, IN 46038
(317) 579-1946

The Polar Bear Express is a wonderful holiday event. It begins with a reading of a railroad–themed Christmas story and takes the families on a roundtrip ride from the Fishers station to the Noblesville Station. Refreshments and visiting with Santa, Mrs. Claus, and the Polar Bear make this a favorite for WonderDad's little ones.

HAMILTON EAST PUBLIC LIBRARY
Fishers

5 Municipal Dr.
Fishers, IN 46038
(317) 579-0300

Call to register for different activities for all ages. Activities include Story time offered twice a day, Craft–a–Story for 4-6 year olds, Toddler Time for 2-3 year olds, Create–a–Story for 5-8 year olds, Read–to–Read program for child and adult, and Bunny Hop for babies. So much more can be found by visiting the library to get a schedule of events.

PINHEADS
Fishers

13825 Britton Park Rd.
Fishers, IN 46038
(317) 773-9988 | www.bowlatpinheads.com

WonderDad and his kids will love bowling here, as well as eating some little snacks in between games. The bowling alley is quite big and has an area with arcade games and air hockey tables. There is an area for little kids as well called "Play A Lot." There is often live music in the evenings for the kids and dads to dance along with.

THE FORUM AT FISHERS
Fishers

9022 E 126th St.
Fishers, IN 46038
(317) 849-9930

The Forum at Fishers is a premier twin indoor ice skating facility featuring a fully equipped Pro Shop, great snacks, and a game arcade for the kids. The Forum at Fishers has Public Skating virtually every day. Bring your own skates or rent them at the facility.

BEECH GROVE BOWL AND PIZZA
Indy E

95 N 2nd Ave.
Beech Grove, IN 46107
(317) 784-3743

No matter if your family is up all night or early in the morning, you can go bowling anytime. 24–hours–a–day with fresh pizza available. Any time is a great time to bowl here without worrying about the hours of operation.

BEECH GROVE PUBLIC LIBRARY
Indy E

1102 Main St.
Beech Grove, IN 46107
(317) 788-9203

Preschool story time is on Thursdays at 11am. Other special events take place, so call or visit the library to find out about more fun stuff to do here.

FRANKLIN LIBRARY
Indy E

5550 S Franklin Rd.
Indianapolis, IN 46239
(317) 275-4380

Baby Lapsit Times are on Thursdays at 10:15am. Preschool Story Times are on Wednesdays at 10:15am and 1:15pm. Get more information on other activities by visiting the children's section of the library.

FUN WORLD
Indy E

10202 E Washington St.
Indianapolis, IN 46229
(317) 286-8365

Bounce houses, suited sumo–wrestling, and laser tag are here in Washington Square Mall for WonderDad and kids to enjoy after shopping. This is a great location in the mall because dads come here to shop and the kids will get bored.

INDIANAPOLIS SPEEDROME
Indy E

802 Kitley Ave.
Indianapolis, IN 46219
(317) 353-8206 | www.speedrome.com

This is the home of the world figure–8 tracks in racing. Stock car racing takes place on Friday and Saturday nights from April to September. Kids 5 and younger are always free, so this makes a cheap date for WonderDad and his young ones. There may be age or height requirements for riding on the go-carts and bumper cars, so call ahead to see if the kids are able to do the activities outside or not.

MCDONALD'S
Indy E

7229 E Washington St.
Indianapolis, IN 46219
(317) 353-2771 | www.mcdonalds.com

Most kids love to eat Happy Meals. Here WonderDad can bring an even bigger smile to their faces because of the indoor play area. There is plenty of climbing up and sliding down for little kids wearing socks to enjoy after eating. This is a great place to have birthday parties for kids under 5 years old because not only is it a simple party to plan for the dads, but Ronald McDonald himself will come to the birthday party! A warning for all dads—prepare to be here longer than 1 hour as this play area is filled with other kids to play with and no one wants to leave! Except maybe the dads who have been watching their kids play for over 2 hours and can not get them down without help from another child.

RASCAL'S FUN ZONE
Indy E

10499 E Washington St.
Indianapolis, IN 46229
(317) 889-4536

There are plenty of fun activities to do here including go–karts, bumper cars, and redemption games. Most kids and dads enjoy the go–karts, but call ahead to see how old the kids have to be before going here and finding out the kids are too little to do the go–karts or even the bumper cars.

ROLLER CAVE
Indy E

8734 E 21st St.
Indianapolis, IN 46219
(317) 898-1817 | www.rollercave.com

Hours change seasonally. This is a state–of–the–art skating facility themed to a cave surrounding. The kids will enjoy the large skating surface, full–service snack bar, lighted dance floor and the huge game room. This is the home of the Bat Cave, Indiana's only slam dunk basketball facility featuring indoor baseball and softball batting cages and an 18-hole miniature golf course.

WARREN PERFORMING ARTS CENTER
Indy E

9500 E 16th St.
Indianapolis, IN 46229
(317) 532-6280

Dads and kids will love the performances they see here such as touring shows, concerts, community theater groups, international off–Broadway–style entertainment. Call for current schedule and for ticket prices.

WATERMAN'S FARM MARKET AND HARVEST FESTIVAL

Indy E

7010 E Raymond St.
Indianapolis, IN 46239
(317) 356-6995

Harvest Festival hours: Daily, 9am-8pm in October. Admission: $4 week-days, $5 weekends, ages 2 and under free. Pony rides: $3. What a great way for WonderDad to show his kids how much fun fall time can be. Admission includes a farm tour hayride to the pumpkin patch, two cornfield mazes, a 1,500-square-foot straw bale maze, a straw mountain for climbing, a tricycle trail for ages 10 and under, plus Bouncy Barnstorm – seven huge inflatables to crawl through, climb up, slide down, and bounce on. Live entertainment weekends including a clown and bands.

BUTLER UNIVERSITY JI HOLCOMB OBSERVATORY AND PLANETARIUM

Indy N

4600 Sunset Ave.
Indianapolis, IN 46208
(317) 940-8333 | www.butler.edu/holcomb-observatory

Look up in the sky, WonderDad, and find stars for your kids here. Show times are Fridays and Saturdays at 7:30pm, but arrive early to be sure to get one of the 60 seats available. Kids will love looking in the sky and seeing stars that can be identified. Call ahead to be sure the Observatory and Planetarium are open, as they are closed on some days during the year due to weather and other special events taking place.

CHILDREN'S MUSEUM OF INDIANAPOLIS

Indy N

3000 N Meridian St.
Indianapolis, IN 46208
(317) 334-3322 | www.childrensmuseum.org

From dinosaurs to carousel rides, this museum will take you all day to see all of the fun and educational exhibits that will make the kids and you ready for bed early. When you enter the museum the kids will stare in awe at the giant water clock. The exhibits all have hands–on activities and there are plenty of cultural areas, science and social studies devoted areas, and other fun places to explore on the five levels inside this museum. Special traveling exhibits come every couple of months. Playscape is an area especially for little ones; there are water tables, sand tables, dress up areas, and lots of imaginary play to be had in this part of the museum. In December, celebrate the holidays by sliding down the Yule slide and see it snow inside! Closed on Mondays from Labor Day until Memorial Day. Free admission on the first Thursday of the month from 5pm-8pm, sponsored by Target.

CINEMA GRILL

Indy N

1289 W 86th St.
Indianapolis IN 46260
(317) 254-8248

Cheap movie tickets with better food that any other movie theater you'll ever go to. Surprises like pizza, ice cream, and french fries, along with traditional popcorn, will fill your little ones tummy as they watch a great movie. Get there a little early to get good seats. This movie theater is located in Greenbriar near CVS and Hot Cakes Emporium.

CLOWES MEMORIAL HALL
OF BUTLER UNIVERSITY

Indy N

4602 Sunset Ave.
Indianapolis, IN 46208
(317) 940-6444 | www.cloweshall.org

Dads and kids will enjoy the experience of seeing such wonderful performances held year around. This 2,100-seat performing arts facility is home of Clowes Presents, the Indianapolis Opera, Butler Ballet, JFCA's Music at Butler, and Broadway Across America-Indianapolis. There are many performances to attend here all year long, so call or visit the website for performance dates, times, and ticket prices.

CROWN HILL CEMETERY

Indy N

700 W 38th St.
Indianapolis, IN 46208
(317) 925-8231 | www.crownhill.org

Crown Hill Cemetery is one of the biggest and best known cemeteries in Indiana. Dads and kids will enjoy touring the Gothic Chapel and the Waiting Station as they explore this historic cemetery. This is the famous resting place for President Benjamin Harrison, poet James Whitcomb Riley, Col. Eli Lilly, and the notorious bank robber, John Dillinger. Guided tours are held year round. Call or visit the website for more details.

INDIANAPOLIS MUSEUM OF ART

Indy N

4000 Michigan Rd.
Indianapolis, IN 46208
(317) 923-1331 | www.inamuseum.org

The museum is a cultural experience for dad and the kids to enjoy together. Acclaimed artwork by artists from around the world and throughout the United States includes paintings, sculptures, prints, photographs, and costumes.

INDIANA STATE FAIR

Indy N

Indianapolis Fairgrounds
1202 E 38th St.
Indianapolis, IN 46205
(317) 927-7500

Held in August every year, this fair brings in the most fun all summer. WonderDads can get unlimited ride bracelets and find anything the kids desire to eat at the various vendors. Most popular food items last year were fried Snicker bars, chocolate bacon, fresh ears of corn, tenderloins, and flavored snow cones. Must also visit the Dairy Barn, the 4-H barn animals, healthy kids building, and attend various activities posted each day. The historic Hook's American Drugstore Museum is located on the fairgrounds and is only open to the public during the Indiana State Fair. For more info on the museum, call (317) 924-5825.

INFO ZONE LIBRARY
(INSIDE THE CHILDREN'S MUSEUM)

Indy N

3000 N Meridian St.
Indianapolis, IN 46208
(317) 275-4430

For WonderDad looking to help make himself and his kids more knowledgeable with computers, Little Bytes is from 10am-12pm on Fridays. Families with preschoolers are invited to practice computer basics, create digital art, and collect a Little Bytes prize card! If the museum wasn't exciting enough all by itself, the library is amazing.

NORA PUBLIC LIBRARY

8625 Guilford Ave.
Indianapolis, IN 46260
(317) 275-4470

Toddler story time is on Tuesdays at 10:30am and Baby story time is on Thursdays at 10:30am. Call for all other family activities that take place—especially the Summer Reading Program which encourages kids to read by offering prizes.

PIKE PUBLIC LIBRARY

6525 Zionsville Rd.
Indianapolis, IN 46260
(317) 575-4480

Story time for Toddlers 18-36 months are on Tuesdays at 10:15am. Preschool story time is on Thursdays at 10:15am. Family story time is on Mondays at 7pm. Other activities take place all year round. Call for more information.

PIRATE'S COVE

Indy N

3421 E 96th St.
Indianapolis, IN 46240
(317) 571-0066

This is an indoor miniature golf course that has 36 holes. WonderDads and kids will love trying to get their ball into the holes, as the course is very creatively done and is not as simple as anyone would think looking at it. It is located right next door to Woodland Bowl.

POTTERY BY YOU

Indy N

2260 W 86th St.
Indianapolis, IN 46260
(317) 337-1263

WonderDad can help his kids create a masterpiece at this pottery store. No experience needed, as the assistants at the store can help anyone at any level create a piece they will love.

BONGO BOY MUSIC

Indy NE

8481 Bash St. #1100
Indianapolis, IN 46250
(317) 595-9065 | www.bongoboymusic.com

Open Mon-Thu 1:30pm-9:30pm and Sat 10am-3pm. There is a free community drum circle for WonderDad and his kids to attend. Call for more information.

BUILD-A-BEAR WORKSHOP

Indy NE

6020 E 82nd St.
Indianapolis, IN 46250
(317) 596-8888

This is a wonderful place to celebrate anything special. WonderDad has to help his kids pick everything out at each station to create their own stuffed animals with outfits and a birth certificate to take home. This is an activity that all kids enjoy doing, so Dad should feel like a hero when it's all done.

CASTLETON SQUARE
MALL FOOD COURT

Indy NE

6020 E 82nd St.
Indianapolis, IN 46250
(317) 849-9993 | www.simonmalls.com

Shop until lunchtime and visit the food court that has a variety of fast food eateries all in one area. Then let the kids squeal and giggle as they climb, slide, and hide in the indoor play area.

43

CLIMB TIME INDY

Indy NE

8750 Corporation Dr.
Indianapolis, IN 46256
(317) 596-3330

Indoor rock climbing is a super activity for older kids. They offer instruction, climbing equipment and gear and even private birthday parties! So hang on and enjoy your climb.

DAVE AND BUSTERS

Indy NE

8350 Castleton Corner Dr.
Indianapolis, IN 46250
(317) 572-2706

Arcade games and good food will make this activity a favorite for WonderDad to share with his older kids. This is a huge place, so there is plenty to do to keep everyone busy.

HINDEL BOWL

Indy NE

6833 Pendleton Pike
Indianapolis, IN 46226
(317) 545-1231 | www.hindelbowl.com

Open everyday and is smoke–free in the bowling alley areas. Wonder-Dads and kids will enjoy using one of the 46 lanes available here. There is also a snack bar to re–energize the kids if they get tired after bowling a few games.

LAWRENCE PUBLIC LIBRARY

Indy NE

7898 Hague Rd.
Indianapolis, IN 46256
(317) 275-4460

Baby and Toddler story time is on Tuesdays at 10:30am. Preschool story time for 3-5 year olds are on Thursdays at 10:30am. Other family activities take place each month, so call the library for more information.

MONKEY JOE'S

Indy NE

5661 E 86th St.
Indianapolis, IN 46250
(317) 842-5437

Safety comes first at Monkey Joe's, starting with the play center being only for kids 12 years and younger. Adults are always free, so WonderDad can assist his children 4 and under. They have a Mini Monkey Zone, which is a separate toddler play area for kids 3 and under to keep the younger kids safe.

44

SNAPPERZ
Indy NE

6002 Sunnyside Rd.
Lawrence, IN 46236
(317) 823-4327

Your kids can play on a four story soft play unit, five amazing themed inflatable climbing structures, a 24-foot Climbing Wall, a Bungee – Trampoline, Cosmic Bowling, and Laser Tag. There is a special area for Wonder-Dad's littlest ones in the toddler area with two toddler inflatable climbing structures to play on. There are more than 45 arcade and redemption games and great snacks at the Snapperz Café.

EAGLE CREEK PARK
Indy NW

7840 W 56th St.
Indianapolis, IN 46254
(317) 327-7110

This is one of the few parks in the area with a real beach to play on. Open in the summer and on weekends in the spring and fall.

FAMILY INDOOR MINI GOLF
Indy NW

3919 Lafayette Rd.
Indianapolis, IN 46254
(317) 329-6464

Dad can bring his kids here for fun, no matter what the weather is like outside.

PIKE PERFORMING ART CENTER
Indy NW

6701 Zionsville Rd.
Indianapolis, IN 46268
(317) 216-5450

Professional tours performed here, including dance, concerts, musical theater and one man shows. Performances run from September to April. Call for show times and prices.

PYRAMID PLAYERS AT BEEF AND BOARDS DINNER THEATER
Indy NW

9301 N Michigan Rd.
Indianapolis, IN 46268
(317) 877-9664

Juice and snack included. Hours are 10am Fridays and 10am and 1pm on Saturdays.

ROYAL PIN LEISURE CENTERS

Indy NW

7420 Michigan Rd.
Indianapolis, IN 46268
(317) 291-1295

This is a great bowling center that offers a variety of special deals throughout the year. They offer gutter buffers, so the kids will have a better chance of hitting the pins when they first start learning how to play.

SKATELAND ROLLER SKATING

Indy NW

3902 N Glen Arm.
Indianapolis, IN 46254
(317) 291-6795

Roller skating can be a great bonding experience for WonderDad and his kids. It requires a lot of balance and hand holding, until the kids can race off without Dad holding on to them.

SWEET DREAMS ROLLER WORLD

Indy NW

3947 Basque Ct.
Indianapolis, IN 46228
(317) 291-5221

This is a roller skating rink that is popular in the neighborhood. Wonder-Dads and kids will enjoy spending time here together.

ANNUAL IRVINGTON HALLOWEEN FESTIVAL

Indy W

5600 W Washington St.
Indianapolis, IN 46241
(317) 713-1100

This festival is held every year right around Halloween. This street–fest takes place in an old neighborhood that dads may have read about in the best-selling book "Devil in the White City."

INDIANA SKATE CO INC

Indy W

7141 W Morris St.
Indianapolis, IN 46241
(317) 549-1622

Skateboarding rink for Dad and his older kids to enjoy doing together.

PUMP IT UP!

Indy W

5777 Decatur Blvd.
Indianapolis, IN 46241
(317) 821-1555

Pop in times Monday 10-11:30am and Wednesday and Thursday 12-1:30pm. Family Jump Tuesdays and Thursdays 6:30 pm - 8 pm. This is a great place for the kids to jump and bounce around and burn off some energy.

SPEEDWAY PUBLIC LIBRARY

Indy W

5633 W 25th St.
Indianapolis, IN 46224
(317) 243-8959 | www.speedway.lib.in.us
Spend the morning looking at new books and hearing a story or two. Toddler time (3-4 year olds) is 10am and Toddler Time (0-2 years old) is 10:30am on Tuesdays.

WAYNE BRANCH LIBRARY

Indy W

98 S. Girls School Rd.
Indianapolis, IN 46231
(317) 275-4530
Baby Steps Story time is at 10:30am on Thursdays. Other activities occur monthly, especially in the summer time, so call for more information.

WESTSIDE FUN PARK

Indy W

6430 W 37th St.
Indianapolis, IN 46224
(317) 293-8200
WonderDads and kids will enjoy all the activities available inside and outside at this park. Recreation center with arcade games, go–carts, racecars, and baseball and softball batting ranges.

ADRIAN ORCHARDS

Southport

500 W Epler Ave.
Indianapolis, IN 46217
(317) 784-7783
Hours: Mon-Sat, 9 am-7pm; Sun, noon-6 pm. Pick a variety of apples from this family owned orchard. Dad and kids will both enjoy having apple cider and picking out some other homemade goodies.

CHUCK E. CHEESE'S

Southport

8804 US 31 S
Indianapolis, IN 46227
(317) 887-0646
This is the ideal place for WonderDad and his kids no matter what the weather is like outside. There are redemption games, a huge climbing structure that has slides, tunnels and offers a view from near the ceiling of the restaurant. For the younger kids, there are some little rides and a special play area to keep them from being stepped on by all the kids running in and out. Also has an animated animal that is kids–sized that talks and sings onstage.

47

GOLF DOME & THE ROCK Southport

2106 E National Ave.
Indianapolis, IN 46227
(317) 786-2663 | www.golfdome.us

Golf Dome and The Rock is an indoor sports facility for indoor practice for all Year-Round fun for dads and kids. Target Golf is also available at specific times and dates. Call for more information.

INCREDIBLE PIZZA COMPANY Southport

8707 Hardegan St.
Indianapolis, IN 46227
(317) 644-0153

Pizza buffet, salad bar, soup bar, baked potato bar, taco bar, and a dessert bar will be a winner for hungry WonderDads and children under 6 years old. Before and after eating there is the Comfyland Developmental Area for ages 1-6 to play in.

LONG'S BAKERY Southport

2301 Southport Rd.
Indianapolis, IN 46227
(317) 783-1442

For the best donuts in the state come early and bring home a dozen or more. Wake up the kids and munch on the treats as the sun rises to start a beautiful day.

PERRY ICE RINK Southport

451 E Stop 11 Rd.
Indianapolis, IN 46227
(317) 865-1833

WonderDads and kids can enjoy this indoor skating rink open from October to April. Dads may need to brush up on ice skating before taking their kids out on the ice.

SHELBY BOWL Southport

3808 Shelby St.
Indianapolis, IN 46227
(317) 786-6877

This is a classic family operated bowling alley, so there are only 12 lanes. WonderDad should call about all the specials they offer during the week and weekend.

48

SOUTHPORT LIBRARY

Southport

2630 E Stop 11 Rd.
Indianapolis, IN 46227
(317) 275-4510

Preschool story time is on Tuesdays at 11am and Toddler Tales is on Thursdays at 11am. Call for more details on what else is taking place at the library that dads and kids might enjoy.

SOUTHPORT PUTT-PUTT

Southport

1936 E Southport Rd.
Indianapolis, IN 46227
(317) 787-4852

Miniature golf is a great way for dad and kids to spend some time together outside. Dad can help his younger ones with their hand – eye coordination by playing this activity.

THE BEST DAD/CHILD
STORES

A TASTE OF INDIANA
Broad Ripple

6404 Rucker Rd.
Indianapolis, IN 46220
(317) 252-5850
Custom-created gift baskets filled with unique Indiana products.

BEBE GATE
Broad Ripple

920 Broad Ripple Ave.
Indianapolis, IN 46220
(317) 255-2323 | www.bebegateindy.com
Dads can find a selection of children's clothing and baby apparel.

BIG HATS BOOKS
Broad Ripple

6510 Cornell Ave.
Indianapolis, IN 46220
(317) 202-0203 | www.bighatbook.com
Unique bookstore is sure to be a hit with both WonderDads and kids. With such a great selection in this friendly place, you can't go wrong.

BROAD RIPPLE STATION
Broad Ripple

6675 N College Ave.
Indianapolis, IN 46220
(317) 731-6581
WonderDads and kids who love trains will want to visit this store to see a variety of trains.

CHELSEA'S
Broad Ripple

902 E Westfield Blvd.
Indianapolis, IN 46220
(317) 251-0600
This a funky gift store with lots of cool gifts for the kids to choose for friends' or siblings' birthday presents.

GAME STATION
Broad Ripple

1045 Broad Ripple Ave.
Indianapolis, IN 46220
(317) 253-1434
WonderDad can find many different games for his kids at this store.

GOOD EARTH NATURAL FOOD STORE
Broad Ripple

6350 N Guilford Ave.
Indianapolis, IN 46220
(317) 253-3709

This store offers a broad selection of natural and organic foods, supplements, beauty products, and apparel. They also sell On Earth Footwear, the Birkenstock family of brands, and Haflinger.

HILLSIDE CERAMICS AND GIFTS
Broad Ripple

5621 Hillside Ave.
Indianapolis, IN 46220
(317) 255-4575

Create your own gift of pottery or buy a gift already made; either way your gift is sure to be unique and treasured.

INDIANAPOLIS ART CENTER GIFT SHOP
Broad Ripple

820 E 67th St.
Indianapolis, IN 46220
(317) 255-2464 | www.indplsartcenter.org

Local artwork for sale here, so a one-of-a-kind gift is possible.

INDY CD AND VINYL
Broad Ripple

806 Broad Ripple Ave.
Indianapolis, IN 46220
(317) 259-1012 | www.indydcandvinyl.com

This store has a huge selection of CDs, 45s, imports, posters, and DVDs. If WonderDad is looking for an old favorite band, he's sure to find it here.

SULLIVAN'S HARDWARE STORE
Broad Ripple

6955 N Keystone Ave.
Indianapolis, IN 46220
(317) 255-9230

Need some tools or screws to hang a new picture frame up in a room? This store has all the supplies a handy WonderDad can need to fix toilets, doors, walls, and even the outside of the house!

TEEKI HUT
Broad Ripple

807 Broad Ripple Ave.
Indianapolis, IN 46220
(317) 205-3589

Make your own T-shirt at this unique store, both a great gift for dads and kids to give to others or for themselves.

53

THE BIKE LINE
Broad Ripple

6520 Cornell Ave.
Indianapolis, IN 46220
(317) 253-2611

Need a new bike for either you or your kids? This store has a great selection of bikes for serious bicyclists.

CAPSTONE CAFÉ AND BOOKSTORE
Carmel

12900 Hazel Dell Pkwy.
Carmel, IN 46033
(317) 566-9132

WonderDad can sip some coffee as he and the kids browse the great selection of books offered at this store.

CARMEL BABY BOUTIQUE
Carmel

1370 S Range Line Rd.
Carmel, IN 46032
(317) 816-0100

This store has everything dad needs for his littlest ones—clothes, furniture, and accessories.

CELEBRITY KIDS PORTRAIT STUDIO
Carmel

4300 Clay Terrace Blvd.
Carmel, IN 46032
(317) 846-7827

Celebrity Kids Portrait Studios specializes in children's and family artistic photography. So get some big smiles on the kids' faces and present the pictures to family and friends as holiday gifts.

CRAZY 8
Carmel

14300 Clay Terrace Blvd.
Carmel, IN 46032
(317) 581-8864

This store is a great place to find clothing for boys and girls. Especially your 8 year olds, who seem to be staining their clothes every time you look away.

DECOR 4 KIDS
Carmel

3207 Eden Way
Carmel, IN 46033
(317) 846-4543

Dads can find custom made furniture for his kids' bedrooms. This store specializes in doing rooms for kids, so they are used to creative challenges.

ELITE KIDZ STOP

3626 Patriot Ct.
Carmel, IN 46032
(317) 873-1457

This store has a variety of clothing and accessories for boys and girls. With a great staff and fun stuff its a great back-to-school stop.

GIFTS TO GO BY BASKET CASE   Carmel

14300 Clay Terrace Blvd.
Carmel, IN 46032
(317) 846-5272

Greeting card assortment, baby gift area, bulk chocolate by The South Bend Chocolate Company, and much more.

GYMBOREE STORE   Carmel

4300 Clay Terrace Blvd.
Carmel, IN 46032
(317) 575-0617 | www.gymboree.com

This is a clothing store for newborns, toddlers, and boys and girls up to size 12, full of bright colors and great fashions.

KEEN CHILDREN'S SHOES   Carmel

20 Executive Dr.
Carmel, IN 46032
(317) 580-1830

This is a great little shoe store in Carmel that specializes in children's shoes. They have great customer service and can answer any questions WonderDad may have about which shoes to buy for his kids.

KITS & KABOODLE   Carmel

2442 E 146th St.
Carmel, IN 46033
(317) 566-8108

Unique toys for every age. A great place for finding something special for WonderDad's kids.

MYSTERY CO.   Carmel

233 2nd Ave. SW
Carmel, IN 46032
(317)705-9711

WonderDads and kids who love mysteries will want to visit this local favorite book store.

55

PLAY IT AGAIN SPORTS

Carmel

271 Merchants Square Dr.
Carmel, IN 46032
(317) 848-6044
This is a gently used sports equipment store. They also sell new items like bite guards so WonderDad can find one to keep his kids' teeth safe.

SOCCER VILLAGE

Carmel

1374 S. Range Line Rd.
Carmel, IN 46032
(317) 571-0105
Dads and kids who love to play soccer need to see this store. It has all the equipment and accessories any soccer player could possibly need.

TANGERINE CARDS AND GIFTS

Carmel

4335 W 106th St.
Carmel, IN 46032
(317) 870-1890
This is small gift shop with big surprises for dad and his kids to find.

TEETER TOTTER

Carmel

2454 E 116th St.
Carmel, IN 46032
(317) 566-9291
Dads will find once–in–a–lifetime dresses to buy at this store. They have a variety of beautiful Communion dresses on sale.

THE CREATIVE ESCAPE POTTERY & MOSAIC

Carmel

1366 S Rangeline Rd.
Carmel, IN 46032
(317) 569-8626
WonderDad can help his kids create their own pottery or mosaics.

WHOLE FOODS

Carmel

14300 Clay Terrace Blvd.
Carmel, IN 46032
(317) 569-1517
This store has organic food. It's great healthy choice for dads and kids.

AMERICAN GREETINGS
Downtown

49 W Maryland St.
Indianapolis, IN 46204
(317) 974-0924
WonderDads can bring his kids here to pick out special cards for family and friends.

BROOKSTONE
Downtown

49 W Maryland St.
Indianapolis, IN 46204
(317) 624-9117 | www.brookstone.com
WonderDads and kids will enjoy this store because of its hands–on shopping to discover new and ingenious items of superior quality.

CAMPUS CORNER GIFT SHOP
Downtown

NCAA Hall of Champions, 700 W Washington St.
Indianapolis, IN 46204
(317) 916-4255
This store is filled with sports. Kids will find a selection of items here that they will want to buy after touring the NCAA Hall of Champions.

CAPITOL GIFTS AND GOODIES
Downtown

201 N Illinois St. #180
Indianapolis, IN 46204
(317) 631-2067
This downtown gift store is close to many other attractions and restaurants. WonderDad can find an assortment of goodies to eat and gifts to buy.

COLTS PRO SHOP
Downtown

49 W Maryland St.
Indianapolis, IN 46204
(317) 639-2857
This is the place to find Indianapolis Colts Football team gear for both WonderDad and his kids.

DOWNTOWN COMICS
Downtown

11 E Market St.
Indianapolis, IN 46204
(317) 237-0397
This is a great store to find the best comic books for dads and kids.

STORES

EITELJORG MUSEUM OF AMERICAN INDIANS AND WESTERN ART GIFT SHOP
Downtown

500 W Washington St.
Indianapolis, IN 46204
(317) 636-9378 | www.eiteljorg.org
WonderDad can find Native American–made objects in this gift store.

FAO SCHWARZ
Downtown

49 E Maryland St.
Indianapolis, IN 46204
(317) 636-3500
This store is perfect if you are looking to buy the best stuffed animal you can find for your kids.

FINISH LINE
Downtown

49 W Maryland St.
Indianapolis, IN 46204
(317) 637-2381
This is a great store for athletic WonderDads and kids to find shoes.

FISH BOWL PET CENTER
Downtown

2101 E Michigan St.
Indianapolis, IN 46201
(317) 638-8236
This is the best place to buy your kids first pet—a fish. This center sells all kinds and sizes of aquariums and they are knowledgeable about what fish won't eat other fish.

GARDENER'S PRIDE GIFT STORE
Downtown

White River Gardens, 1200 W Washington St.
Indianapolis, IN 46222
(317) 423-2465
WonderDads and kids who love to play in the dirt will love this store. Anything a gardener might need is all in one place.

GNOSIS GALLERY & GNOSIS: FEED YOUR BEAN
Downtown

1043 Virginia Ave. Suite 5
Indianapolis, IN 46203
(317) 352-0668
Artistic clothing and toys can be found in this store for WonderDads looking for something different to buy their kids.

INDIANA STATE MUSEUM'S
GIFT STORE   Downtown
650 W Washington St.
Indianapolis, IN 46204
(317) 232-1637
There are two floor dedicated to this gift shop. Dads and kids will love
the variety of cool items, especially if they liked the museum's exhibits.

INDIANAPOLIS ZOO'S GIFT STORE   Downtown
1200 W Washington St.
Indianapolis, IN 46222
(317) 630-2001 | www.indyzoo.com
WonderDad can find his kids animals made out of stuffing, paper, wood,
glass, candy, plastic, or even metal.

MASS AVE. TOYS   Downtown
409 Massachusetts Ave. # 201
Indianapolis, IN 46204
(317) 955-8697
Great gifts that are unique and fun can be found here. They have a great
selection of Melissa and Doug Puzzles and activity sets.

NUTURE   Downtown
433 Massachusetts Ave.
Indianapolis, IN 46204
(317) 423-1234
This store sells modern clothing for babies and kids, sizes newborn to 6 years
old.

PACERS HOME COURT II   Downtown
49 W Maryland St.
Indianapolis, IN 46204
(317) 262-9962
WonderDads and kids will find basketball everywhere in this store. This is
the Indianapolis Pacers' store, so you can find plenty of great items with
the Pacers logo on it.

COOKIE CUTTERS   Fisherss
8964 E 96th St.
Fishers, IN 46038
(317) 577-7854
WonderDad can be a hero by bringing his kids here to get their hair cut.
They can watch television or play an electronic game to keep them en-
tertained.

CONNOR PRAIRIE'S GIFT SHOP
Fisherss

13400 Allisonville Rd.
Fishers, IN 46038
(317) 776-6006

Find amazing gifts here, from books to toys from yesteryear and now. They have some pretty jewelry that Wonderdad's kids may want or books on life years ago.

CORNERSTONE GIFTS & BOOKS
Fisherss

7850 E 96th St.
Fishers, IN 46038
(317) 842-8942

This is a gift store that also sells some cool books for dads and kids to look over.

FAIRWAY CUSTOM GOLF
Fisherss

12500 Brooks School Rd.
Fishers, IN 46038
(317) 842-0017

This is a great store to find equipment for golf. Dads will appreciate the selection of clubs, while the kids will like looking at the other accessories.

FISHERS DO IT CENTER
Fisherss

11881 Lakeside Dr.
Fishers, IN 46038
(317) 841-2735

This home improvement store can show the kids what WonderDad needs to do a job around the house.

FRY'S ELECTRONICS
Fisherss

9820 Kincaid Dr.
Fishers, IN 46038
(317) 594-3101 | www.frys.com

This is a huge electronics store and dads can find a variety of items for his kids and himself.

MCNAMARA
Fisherss

8707 N by Northeast Blvd.
Fishers, IN 46038
(317) 579-7900

Best known for being a popular store to buy flowers and have them delivered to family or friends. Inside the store, dads and kids will see a huge variety of gifts as well; many with a country charm feeling to it.

MUDSOCK BOOKS & CURIOSITY SHOP
Fisherss

11850 Allisonville Rd.
Fishers, IN 46038
(317) 579-9822

The kids might enjoy shopping here for books or other little gifts to buy for teachers.

PIPER CHILDREN'S BOUTIQUE
Fisherss

8235 E 116th St.
Fishers, IN 46038
(317) 578-7002

High-end prices for beautiful clothes for kids can be found here.

RADIO SHACK
Fisherss

7830 E 96th St.
Fishers, IN 46038
(317) 570-0697

This is a great electronic store that both WonderDads and kids will love to explore. They have great remote control toys for kids.

THE COLLECTOR'S FRIEND
Fisherss

8775 E 116th St.
Fishers, IN 46038
(317) 845-8938

Looking for something special for the kids to start a collection of? This store has a great assortment of items.

ASHLEY'S GIFT & BASKET CO
Indy E

45 N 6th Ave.
Beech Grove, IN 46107
(317) 788-6511

Looking for a huge quantity of gift baskets? Then visit this store. This is great for dads who need lots of gifts for any occasion.

BARNES & NOBLE
Indy E

10202 E Washington St.
Indianapolis, IN 46229
(317) 899-4150

This is a great bookstore that also has a coffee shop inside of it. The selection of books; paperback or hardcover will allow WonderDad to find something new to read. In the Children's Section, kids can find a variety of books. For example, they have beginning readers and chapter books.

61

CIRCUIT CITY
Indy E

10235 E Washington St.
Indianapolis, IN 46229
(317) 895-0623

This is a great place to find a bigger television set for the family room or to find a new printer for WonderDad's office. Kid's love this store because of the walls of TVs.

COLLECTOR'S PARADISE
Indy E

5618 E Washington St.
Indianapolis, IN 46229
(317) 357-2291

Looking for old editions of your favorite comic books? Then grab the kids and come to paradise.

DICK'S SPORTING GOODS
Indy E

10202 E Washington St.
Indianapolis, IN 46229
(317) 890-8802

Pick up the gear you need for just about any sport the kids want to play at this sporting goods superstore. There is equipment, clothing, and other items in each department, plus the staff is more than happy to help you make informed decisions about what you need for beginners in each sport.

KIDS FOOT LOCKER
Indy E

10202 E Washington St.
Indianapolis, IN 46229
(317) 898-5809

If WonderDad's kids need new shoes, the experts at this store can help them find the best pair.

LIFE CHRISTIAN BOOK STORE
Indy E

10202 E Washington St.
Indianapolis, IN 46229
(317) 890-1418

This store is filled with Christian books and gifts, and is a great place to go to get christening gifts or for other occasions that call for the thoughtful, spiritual gift.

PORTER PAINTS
Indy E

6951 E 30th St.
Indianapolis, IN 46219
(317) 546-5714

WonderDads and kids will find a huge selection of colors to paint any room in the house. They can mix color for you and help you decide if a color would be good on all four walls.

SHOE CARNIVAL
Indy E

10609 E Washington St.
Indianapolis, IN 46229
(317) 890-9520

WonderDads and kids can find a large selection of shoes here. Weekly specials like buy – one – and – get – one – half – price are the best time to visit this store.

THE GLITTERIE
Indy E

506 Main St.
Beech Grove, IN 46107
(317) 786-8149

WonderDads and kids can find scrapbook supplies here for anyone who's making a book. Kids can even get started by creating a scrapbook by having Dad help them select some pages to start their own album.

THE PEANUT GALLERY
Indy E

821 Timber Creek Dr.
Indianapolis, IN 46239
(317) 373-0734

This store sells baby and children's clothing. Dads can find great little dresses for his kids at this store.

THE TRAIN YARD
Indy E

9940 E Washington St,
Indianapolis, IN 46229
(317) 890-9774

Looking for a new train set? Then come in and see what this store has to offer.

TOYS 'R' US
Indy E

9251 E Washington St.
Indianapolis, IN 46229
(317) 897-0320

This store is WonderDad's best place to find Hasbro® products as well as a huge variety of toys, games, books, and so much more!

TRAIN CENTRAL
Indy E

6742 E Washington St.
Indianapolis, IN 46219
(317) 375-0832

WonderDads and kids can both look at a variety of trains at this store. Chug along the aisles to see all of the types of trains and spare parts available for sale.

STORES

63

BEACH BABY SURF & SWIM SHOP
Indy N

8687 River Crossing Rd.
Indianapolis, IN 46240
(317) 574-4945

Dads can buy his little kids beachwear anytime of the year. If the family decides to take a trip in March and the kids' bathing suits are too small, then come to this store where every day is like a beach.

GAME CRAZY
Indy N

3820 N College Ave.
Indianapolis, IN 46205
(317) 925-4268

Video gamers will find a variety of games and accessories in this store.

INDIANA MUSEUM OF ART GIFT STORE
Indy N

4000 Michigan Rd.
Indianapolis, IN 46208
(317) 923-1331 | www.inamuseum.org

Reproductions of the artwork on display can be found in postcards at this museum shop.

JANIE AND JACK
Indy N

8702 Keystone Crossing
Indianapolis, IN 46240
(317) 575-6115 | www.janieandjack.com

Detailed designers clothes for girls and boys up to size 6.

KIDS INK CHILDREN'S STORE
Indy N

5619 N Illinois
Indianapolis, IN 46208
(317) 253-2598

Children's bookstore that has a great selection of books, WonderDads will be able to find a great book for their young reader.

KILLYBEGS IRISH SHOP
Indy N

1300 E 86th St.
Indianapolis, IN 46240
(317) 846-9449

A great gift shop filled with the luck of the Irish.

PAMPOLINA
Indy N

8702 Keystone Crossing
Indianapolis, IN 46240
(317) 575-1990

Pampolina's European edge is hip and unique with an extraordinary eye for details and sells clothes for boys and girls.

PAPYRUS
Indy N

8702 Keystone Crossing
Indianapolis, IN 46240
(317) 573-9040

They sell an ever-expanding array of products including greeting cards, gift wrap, gift bags, stationery, note cards, journals, Marcel Schurman Creations and unique gift products.

POTTERY BARN FOR KIDS
Indy N

8702 Keystone Crossing
Indianapolis, IN 46240
(317) 569-9144

Pottery Barn Kids offers quality home furnishings for the little ones in your life. WonderDads will feel good shopping here because Pottery Barn Kids' design is guided by a careful regard for child safety standards.

SWEET THINGS CANDY & GIFTS
Indy N

2288 W 86th St.
Indianapolis, IN 46260
(317) 872-8720

WonderDads can find a variety of sweet items here to buy for Mother's Day. They also have nice gifts that can be given along with the chocolates to the woman he loves.

THE CHILDREN'S MUSEUM GIFT STORE
Indy N

3000 N Meridian St.
Indianapolis, IN 46208
(317) 334-3322 | www.childrensmuseum.org

This is one of the best stores to find unique gifts for WonderDad's kids who love anything science related.

65

WOODEN KEY GIFT & CARD SHOP   Indy N

1300 E 86th St.
Indianapolis, IN 46240
(317) 815-1833
This store is located all across Indiana because of all the great gift items WonderDad and his kids can find there.

GAP KIDS   Indy NE

6020 E 82nd St.
Indianapolis, IN 46250
(317) 842-1261
Children's clothing store for boys and girls. This store has clothes that will fit dad's kids under 10, but as they get older they can move up into shopping at the regular GAP Store.

HALLMARK   Indy NE

6020 E 82nd St.
Indianapolis, IN 46250
(317) 849-7631
WonderDad will find an assortment of cards to send to loved ones here. They have a selection of figurines that are quite popular as gifts.

HEIDELBERG HAUS   Indy NE

7625 Pendleton Pike
Indianapolis, IN 46226
(317) 547-1230 | www.heidelberghaus.com
German café grocery, antiques, bakery, and gift store. This is a great place to introduce the kids to German culture.

LEGO STORE   Indy NE

Castleton Square Mall
6020 E 82nd St.
Indianapolis, IN 46250
This store is Lego® heaven for kids and big–kid WonderDads. There is a special "pick–a–Brick" section. Kids will also be able to choose from a variety of pieces to build their own customized Lego® mini-figures. The first Tuesday of each month, the first 250 kids (under 14 years old) to come into the store get a free set of Legos®! Opens in early April 2011.

MATTHEW'S BICYCLES   Indy NE

7272 Pendleton Pike
Indianapolis, IN 46226
(317) 547-3456
WonderDads and kids will find a huge variety of bikes here; from unicycles to the rare 4-wheeled variety! The staff is friendly and can help dads decide what bike would work best for his kids based on age and ability.

SKIER'S EDGE
Indy NE

7213 E 87th St.
Indianapolis, IN 46250
(317) 841-1234

WonderDads and kids who love water sports all year long will want to shop at this store. They have everything you need—water, snow, and skateboards, water skis, wakeboards, snowboards, and all the sportswear you'll need to do any of these activities!

THE DISNEY STORE
Indy NE

6020 E 82nd St.
Indianapolis, IN 46250
(317) 578-0335

If WonderDad is looking to buy anything made by Disney, including stuffed animals, videos, costumes, and much more, then he has found the best store for him in the area.

THE LEARNING SHOP
Indy NE

6368 E 82nd St.
Indianapolis, IN 46250
(317) 842-1723

Educational store with a huge selection of musical CDs that teach kids a variety of information from the ABCs to learning a new language.

THE PICTURE PEOPLE
Indy NE

6020 E 82nd St.
Indianapolis, IN 46250
(317) 915-1630

Picture People's stores are full of one-of-a-kind props and colorful backdrops. The best thing about the store is that the pictures of the kids are done in an hour.

THE PRO SHOP
Indy NE

6020 E 82nd St.
Indianapolis, IN 46250
(317) 849-3692

Looking for a place to buy your kids their first golf clubs? WonderDad can drop by this store and find all sizes of clubs for his kids or for himself.

UNITED ARTS AND EDUCATION
Indy NE

8265 Center Run Dr.
Indianapolis, IN 46256
(317) 849-2725

This is where teachers buy many of the activities they use in the classroom. WonderDad can find a gift for his kids' teachers or shop for new games, toys, books, art materials, and learning activities to do at home.

STORES

67

UNIVERSITEES BY T.I.S.
Indy NE

6020 E 82nd St.
Indianapolis, IN 46250
(317) 842-2411

Even very small athletic kids can find their own sports teams on a shirt that will fit them.

VINTAGE NATURAL FOODS
Indy NE

7391 N Shadeland Ave.
Indianapolis, IN 46250
(317) 842-1032

Best place for vitamins & knowledge. Specializing in nutrition, i.e. protein powders, vitamins & minerals, cutting–edge nutrients and hard–to–find nutraceuticals. Wheat–free & gluten–free products available.

YOUNG CHILDREN'S BOOKS
Indy NE

3935 W Franklin Rd. #316
Indianapolis, IN 46226
(317) 701-6753

A small bookstore filled with young children's books is a place Wonder-Dad might want to sneak over and check out before taking his kids there.

ATHLETICS SPORTING GOODS
Indy NW

7168 Zionsville Rd.
Indianapolis, IN 46268
(317) 295-1250

This sporting goods store has a variety of items that all kids and dads can use, no matter what sport they are into playing.

BOOKS A MILLION
Indy NW

5750 W 86th St.
Indianapolis, IN 46278
(317) 876-3668 | www.booksamillioninc.com

Books, books, and more books are here for WonderDad and his kids to search.

CREATION STATION LLC.
Indy NW

5888 W 71st St.
Indianapolis, IN 46278
(317) 291-8444

This store is famous for its own line of figures called "Be'an Collectables." They have a huge selection of religious, historical, collegiate, and exclusive types for WonderDads to buy for his kids or for a special teacher for the end of the year gift.

4 KIDS BOOKS
Indy NW

4450 Weston Pointe Dr. #120,
Zionsville, IN 46077
(317) 733-8710

A wonderful cozy store filled with toys, books, and activities for kids of all ages. Dads can find this store going just north of Carmel on Michigan Rd. to a side street.

GAMESTOP
Indy NW

3319 E 86th St.
Indianapolis, IN 46268
(317) 475-0122 | www.GameStop.com

This store sells the most popular new software, hardware and game accessories for the PC and next generation game console systems from Sony, Nintendo, Microsoft, and Sega. WonderDads and kids will be pleased that it is also the industry's largest reseller of pre-played games.

JUSTICE
Indy NW

6010 W 86th St. Suite 104
Indianapolis, IN 46278
(317) 334-0552

Justice is a trendy store for girls of all ages. WonderDad can find clothes and accessories for his princesses here.

LOWE'S HOME IMPROVEMENT
Indy NW

8440 Michigan Rd.
Indianapolis, IN 46268
(317) 875-7500

Once a month, on a Saturday, there are small projects for dad and his kids to complete in the store. An example of one project done was birdhouses.

OLD NAVY
Indy NW

5910 W 86th St.
Indianapolis, IN 46278
(317) 337-0893

Clothes for WonderDad's entire family can be found here for great prices. Talking mannequins seen in television commercials are Old Navy's trademark right now.

STRIDE RITE
Indy NW

2902 W 86th St.
Indianapolis, IN 46268
(317) 228-1200

This shoe store is the place to go when Dad's little ones start to walk. They have the smallest shoes and can help you find a pair that fits your toddler perfectly.

STORES

69

STORES

TRADER JOE'S
Indy NW

2902 W 86th St.
Indianapolis, IN 46268
(317) 337-1880

A unique food store that can help dads find anything if he or his kids are on a special diet. They have frozen and fresh baked goods available as well.

BATTERIES PLUS
Indy W

4435 Lafayette Rd.
Indianapolis, IN 46254
(317) 293-3555

WonderDads can find the biggest selection of batteries at this store. If you bring in your watch, they will take the old battery out and put the new one in for you!

BLOCKBUSTER VIDEO
Indy W

5748 Crawfordsville Rd.
Indianapolis, IN 46234
(317) 244-3415

This is a great store for renting or even buying newly released movies on DVD. WonderDads and kids will love the selection of movies and video games that can be rented.

EB GAMES
Indy W

6905 S Emerson Ave.
Indianapolis, IN 46237
(317) 788-4602

This is a great store to buy or trade in new games for all the hottest gaming systems.

HAT WORLD
Indy W

3919 Lafayette Rd.
Indianapolis, IN 46254
(317) 347-1105

This store has a great selection of hats. Find your favorite sports team logo here for WonderDads and kids.

KINGDOM MAGIC
Indy W

9240 Crawfordsville Rd
Indianapolis, IN 46234
(317) 298-4137

This is a magic shop filled with great tricks for WonderDads and kids to perform. Find simple magic tricks to more difficult ones to perform in front of any audience.

MENARDS
Indy W

6450 Gateway Dr.
Indianapolis, IN 46254
(317) 297-7458

WonderDads can save money by shopping at this store for his items on his to–do lists. There are aisles full of materials and the staff members are always around to help you find what you are looking for.

RAINBOW KIDS
Indy W

3919 Lafayette Rd.
Indianapolis, IN 46254
(317) 295-9194

This store is a colorful clothing store for all kids. Dads will be sure to find some nice school clothes for his kids here.

SPEEDWAY HANDMADE BICYCLE WORKS
Indy W

1432 Main St.
Indianapolis, IN 46224
(317) 731-4040

This store will help WonderDads and kids make their bikes original. They make bikes according to what the customer wants; from color to the size, each bike is unique.

THE CHILDREN'S PLACE
Indy W

3919 Lafayette Rd.
Indianapolis, IN 46254
(317) 291-0070

This is a clothing store for boys and girls of all ages. WonderDads will be able to find holiday clothes for his kids to wear on special occasions.

THE DUGOUT
Indy W

5707 W Morris St.
Indianapolis, IN 46241
(317) 247-5158

This store sells sports–related items. Kids can find some Yu–Gi–Oh cards along side the baseball cards, but that is an exception.

UNCLE BILL'S PET STORE
Indy W

4829 W 38th St.
Indianapolis, IN 46254
(317) 291-3344

This is a great store if dad wants to buy a pet for his kids. WonderDad should buy them a fish or a bird, as these are easier to maintain than a cat or dog for young children.

71

STORES

WELLINGTON'S WORLD
Indy W

5835 Beaufort Ln.
Indianapolis, IN 46254
(317) 297-5578

This is a gift shop with a variety of items to purchase. WonderDads and kids can browse through cards and many small items.

BABIES 'R' US
Southport

8800 US Hwy 31 S
Indianapolis, IN 46227
(317) 885-7700

WonderDads will be able to find everything from furniture to diapers for his youngest kids at this store. They have great baby gifts and a great selection of car seats and strollers.

BATH AND BODY WORKS
Southport

4850 E Southport Rd # C
Indianapolis, IN 46237
(317) 788-2811 | www.bathandbodyworks.com

WonderDad can bring his kids here to find a special gift for any female; body lotions, candles, bath accessories, and other great smelling products can be found here.

BORDERS
Southport

7565 US Hwy 31 S
Indianapolis, IN 46227
(317) 859-2949

A huge bookstore filled with top-selling books and a big area for children. The children's section offers books of all kinds and games for children of all ages.

COMIC CARNIVAL
Southport

7311 US Hwy 31 S.
Indianapolis, IN 46227
(317) 889-8899

Comic book lovers will be delighted to see the selection at this store. WonderDads and kids both will find comic books that they can read and share.

CRACKER BARREL OLD COUNTRY STORE
Southport

4350 E Southport Rd.
Indianapolis, IN 46237
(317) 784-7691

This is a store inside a restaurant with good food, but the store has an amazing selection of gifts and old fashion stick candies are a winner with dads.

HOBBY TOWN USA
Southport

7765 S US Highway 31
Indianapolis, IN 46227
(317) 882-3175

WonderDad and his kids can find a variety of activities to do together at this store. The coolest item is a rocket that launches 1000ft in the air.

MICHAEL'S ARTS & CRAFT STORE
Southport

8030 US Hwy 31 S
Indianapolis, IN 46227
(317) 882-3266

Looking for poster board or a new picture frame? Then come visit this huge art store that has activities for all ages; paints, scrapbooks, model airplane books, beads to make jewelry, and a big selection of kids' rainy day activities they can do when WonderDad can't take them outside.

THE HOME DEPOT
Southport

4850 E Southport Rd.
Indianapolis, IN 46237
(317) 780-8881

Bring the kids along to find supplies to help WonderDad do some house projects. Watch out for them trying to sneak a ride on one of the large rolling carts!

USA PARTY SUPPLIES INC.
Southport

7257 US Hwy 31 S
Indianapolis, IN 46227
(317) 889-017

WonderDads can get all the birthday supplies they need at this huge store. They have party favors, decorations, wrapping paper, and a whole lot more!

THE BEST DAD/CHILD
OUTDOOR PARKS & RECREATION

ARTS PARK
Broad Ripple

820 E 67th St.
Indianapolis, IN 46220
(317) 255-2464 | www.indplsartcenter.org

A creative outside park filled with sculptures and other beautiful artwork.
This is a great place for WonderDads and kids on a sunny day to explore
all the various artwork outside.

BROAD RIPPLE PARK
Broad Ripple

1550 Broad Ripple Ave.
Indianapolis, IN 46220
(317) 327-7161 | www.indyparks.com

WonderDad can bring his loved ones here to play. The dog park is located next to the playgrounds. This is Broad Ripple's biggest park and has
great playgrounds, an outside pool open in the summer with a lifeguard,
and a recreation center.

BROAD RIPPLE POOL
Broad Ripple

1610 Broad Ripple Ave.
Indianapolis, IN 46220
(317) 327-7333

WonderDad and the kids can jump and splash at this outdoor pool in the
summer. Call for hours and more information.

CANTERBURY PARK
Broad Ripple

5510 N Carvel Ave.
Indianapolis, IN 46220
(317) 327-7461

Park sits on three acres bordering the Monon Trail. There is a playground
(ADA accessible) with swing sets and a sand volley ball court. Wonder-
Dads and kids will enjoy walking as well as playing on the playground
at this park.

CAREY GROVE PARK
Carmel

14001 N Carey Rd.
Carmel, IN 46033
(317) 571-4144 | www.carmelclayparks.com

WonderDad and his kids can work up a sweat at this park. The park has Arbo-
retum basketball court (1/2 size), a community garden, picnic areas, a
softball diamond, and two different playgrounds to play on. The kids can
practice shooting baskets or climb on both of the playgrounds with WonderDad standing nearby or playing as well.

COOL CREEK PARK
Carmel

2000 E 151st St.
Carmel, IN 46033
(317) 896-3528

This beautiful park has plenty of activities to offer for all the changing seasons. Wooded trails span 3-4 miles of wildlife and nature in their peaceful natural settings, and allow for the Nature Center to be a busy place. The park has a huge playground with restrooms and drinking fountains close by. No matter what time of day you come, there will be at least 5 other families there. WonderDad and his kids will enjoy taking a walk in this park. The walking trails go through the woods, over bridges, and past a small creek that runs through most of the park.

LAWRENCE W. INLOW PARK
Carmel

6310 Main St.
Carmel, IN 46032
(317) 571-4144 | www.carmelclayparks.com

This is one of the best parks in Carmel because it has a community garden, playgrounds, three treehouse play structure playgrounds, restrooms, nature trails, water feature/spray park (interactive fountain), and plenty of shelters and picnic tables. Many WonderDads and kids love playing in this park for hours, so bring plenty of sunscreen for the hot sunny days!

RIVER HERITAGE PARK
Carmel

11813 River Rd.
Carmel, IN 46033
(317) 571-4144 | www.carmelclayparks.com

WonderDads and kids will enjoy this park. It has an amphitheater, a picnic area, a great playground ("Everybody's Playground," an interactive, adaptive playground for those with special needs), restrooms, two sand volleyball courts and a picnic area with shelters. Special events are held here during the summer.

WEST PARK
Carmel

2700 W 116th St.
Carmel, IN 46032
(317) 571-4144 | www.carmelclayparks.com

This is a big park with lots of activities to do. The best thing is that Wonder-Dad can bring his kids any time of the year and find activities to do here. There is no reason to worry about the snow or the hot humidity. The park has a picnic area, a big playground, a Prairie garden, restrooms, a cool Sledding Hill Trail (2.5 mile), water feature/spray park (interactive, farm-themed,) wetland pond, and boardwalk (5 acres) to enjoy. Drive by in the winter and you can see all the bundled–up kids sledding down the hill. Drive by in the summer with your window down and you can hear laughter as the kids splash each other with water.

BROOKSIDE PARK   Downtown

3500 Brookside Parkway S Dr.
Indianapolis, IN 46201
(317) 327-7179

This downtown Indianapolis Park has a lot to offer WonderDads and kids. There is an aquatic center, playgrounds, basketball and tennis courts, disc golf course, and a family center with auditorium, weight room, and game room. WonderDads and kids can spend hours here inside or outside.

DOUGLAS PARK   Downtown

1616 E 25th St.
Indianapolis, IN 46218
(317) 327-7174

There is a family center at this park that offers programs and activities for families during the year. The kids will love the outdoor pool, after they have played on the playground first. Dads and kids who love to play sports will enjoy the rest of the areas in the park like the picnic shelters, baseball and softball diamonds, tennis courts, basketball courts, football field, and fitness trail.

GARFIELD PARK   Downtown

2345 Pagoda Dr.
Indianapolis, IN 46203
(317) 327-7220 | www.garfieldparkindy.org

Beautiful gardens are all over in this huge and popular downtown park. Has a 3-tiered pagoda for visitors to view downtown Indianapolis. Also has a horseshoe court, walking trails, playground, and a great sledding hill for enjoying the winter snow.

INDY CANAL WALK
WHITE RIVER STATE PARK   Downtown

Canal level 429 W Ohio St.
Indianapolis, IN 46202
(317) 767-5072 | www.indycanalwalk.org

This is an adventure for WonderDads and kids to see downtown by land or water. Rent bikes, pedal boats, Segways, or let a gondolier steer you down the canal. White River runs through Indianapolis and can be seen from many area attractions.

MUNICIPAL GARDEN FAMILY CENTER
Downtown

1831 Lafayette Rd.
Indianapolis, IN 46222
(317) 327-7190

This park is a great place to cool off in the summer's heat for WonderDads and kids. The park has a playground, splash park, gymnasium, picnic shelter, and outdoor basketball courts. The splash park is a favorite for local kids in the area.

BILLERICAY
Fisherss

12690 Promise Rd.
Fishers, IN 46038
(317) 595-3150

WonderDad's little ones eagerly anticipate a playground visit while a soothing stroll through the woods via the multi-use trail is good at any age. The splash pad is open from Memorial Day weekend to Labor Day from 10am-8pm daily.

CYNTHEANNE PARK
Fisherss

12383 Cyntheanne Rd.
Fishers, IN 46037
(317) 595-3150

This park has two separate playground areas (ages 2-5 and 5-12) plus many natural-area grass trails and public restrooms. WonderDad can feel safe knowing that his kids are playing on age appropriate playgrounds.

ELLER FIELDS
Fisherss

10198 Eller Rd.
Fishers, IN 46038
(317) 595-3150

WonderDad can find baseball and softball diamonds with lighted fields. Concessions and vending machines offer snacks for hungry kids. Playground areas in the park are close to the restrooms, so WonderDad does not have to worry about anyone having an accident while playing.

HARRISON THOMPSON PARK
Fisherss

13573 Conner Knoll Pkwy.
Fishers, IN 46038
(317) 595-3150

A walk on the trail loosens limbs morning or evening, and nothing tastes quite like a grilled burger eaten with family under the picnic shelter, prepared as your kids swing high on the playground. WonderDad will find many local families in the area at the park when he brings his kids to play here.

OUTDOOR PARKS

OLIO FIELDS
Fisherss

14181 E 126th St.
Fishers, IN 46037
(317) 595-3150

This is a baseball lover's place to visit with a concession building, lighted baseball and softball fields, playground areas, and public restrooms. On the weekends, WonderDads and kids can watch a game or play on the playground equipment.

FORT HARRISON STATE PARK
Indy E

5753 Glenn Rd.
Indianapolis, IN 46216
(317) 591-0904

This is a National State Park and is huge! The park has so many things for families to do together; bike trails, fishing, hiking, and the nature center. Many activities are available, so WonderDad should call ahead and see what activities or programs are currently available for the kids to enjoy.

INDY ISLAND AQUATIC CENTER
Indy E

8575 E Raymond St.
Indianapolis, IN 46239
(317) 862-6876

If the snow or rain has your kids grumpy, WonderDad can take them to this indoor pool to brighten up their day. This center is indoor pool fun at its best. There are three pools, a waterslide, and a leisure pool with a water playground. Dads and kids will want to play here all afternoon!

SARAH T. BOLTON PARK
Indy E

1300 Churchman Ave.
Beech Grove, IN 46107
(317) 788-4984

This is one of the three parks located in Beech Grove and is the best one for kids. There are nice playgrounds located here, but the best feature of the park is the skateboarding section. This is one of the few parks to offer ramps and space exclusive to skateboard in. The kids will be amazed at the local kids skateboarding and doing tricks if they are unable to skateboard yet.

WASHINGTON PARK
Indy E

3130 E 30th St.
Indianapolis, IN 46219
(317) 327-7175

This park has a huge family center with a gymnasium, a fitness room, a game room, and a computer lab. Outside of the family center lays the rest of the park, which has even more fun activities for dads and kids. There is a disc golf course, basketball courts, nature walking trails, and the best part; a playground for the kids.

WINDSOR VILLAGE PARK
Indy E

6510 E 25th St.
Indianapolis, IN 46219
(317) 327-7162

WonderDads and kids can enjoy using the family center which has a fitness room, multi–use community room, and a computer lab. Outside in the park, there are basketball courts, a playground, sprayground, and walking trails.

ARSENAL PARK
Indy N

1400 E 46th St.
Indianapolis, IN 46205
(317) 327-7806

This 12.32-acre park has some of the most beautiful trees in the city. Pack a lunch for everyone and enjoy a warm day. Enjoy the spray pool, playground, and picnic shelters on hot summer days.

ELWOOD AND MARY BLACK PARK
Indy N

4241 Fairview Terr.
Indianapolis, IN 46208
(317) 327-7461

The park sits on 2 acres in the middle of the community surrounding Butler University. The beautiful green space provides ample opportunity for passive recreation with one swing set.

HOLLIDAY PARK
Indy N

6363 Springmill Rd.
Indianapolis, IN 46260
(317) 327-7180

Local dads and kids love coming to this park, especially when special events are taking place. Best place to go bird watching and then fearlessly going on the rock climbing wall. They also have a playground, nature center, and many walking trails.

100 ACRES: THE VIRGINIA B FAIRBANKS ART AND NATURE CENTER
Indy N

4000 Michigan Rd.
Indianapolis, IN 46208
(317) 293-1331 | www.imamuseum.org

Outside art park with artwork everywhere, trails, and a beautiful lake. Your children will be delighted by the "Funky Bones" exhibit made out of 20 fiberglass benches to create the shape of a skeleton. Kids will enjoy seeking out art while being in a park–like atmosphere.

81

RIVERSIDE AQUATIC CENTER

Indy N

2420 N Riverside Dr.
Indianapolis, IN 46208
(317) 327-7272

WonderDad will love swimming at this pool as much as his kids do. Open from Memorial Day to Labor Day. Park also has indoor and outdoor basketball courts, tennis courts, a fitness trail, picnic shelter, and two playgrounds.

DUBARRY PARK

Indy NE

3698 Dubarry Rd.
Indianapolis, IN 46226
(317) 327-7461

Here you'll find both basketball and tennis courts for WonderDad to teach his young ones. Also in the park are a small pond, a fun playground, and areas dedicated to nature study.

LAWRENCE COMMUNITY PARK

Indy NE

5301 N Franklin Rd.
Indianapolis, IN 46226
(317) 549-4836

This park is filled with activities for everyone in the area to enjoy; no ages are excluded. WonderDad will want to bring his kids here to play on the playground and watch a game of baseball, tennis, volleyball, or soccer. There are special events and activities during the year, so call to get more details. For seniors, the park has a community center where they can play Bingo, cards, games, or take some craft classes.

LEE ROAD PARK

Indy NE

6200 Lee Rd.
Lawrence, IN 46226
(317) 545-7275

The park has a nice playground, many areas for picnicking, and plenty of Fall Creek Little League Baseball games to watch. So WonderDads and kids can come watch a game, or, if they live in the area, sign up to play in the Little League Baseball.

LOUIS J. JENN PARK

Indy NE

10450 E 63rd St.
Lawrence, IN 46226
(317) 545-7275

This is a nice park for WonderDad and his kids to visit to do some fishing. In the water, there are many kinds of tiny fish to be caught by WonderDad or his kids.

VETERAN'S MEMORIAL PARK
Indy NE

12150 E 62nd St.
Lawrence, IN 46226
(317) 545-7275

This is a special park because it has a huge memorial to remember our veterans. Also, the kids can play on the playground or drag WonderDad along the walking trails.

EAGLE CREEK PARK
Indy NW

7840 W 56th St.
Indianapolis, IN 46254
(317) 327-7110

This is a state park that has a 1,350-acre reservoir with 3,900 acres of wooden terrain and open meadows. WonderDads and kids can spend the whole day at this park doing a lot of activities. They can have fun doing these activities: ride on bike trails, walk on footpaths, see the Earth Discovery Center, the Indianapolis Rowing Center, the Marina Music Stage, the Marsh & Bird Sanctuary, the Ornithology Center, the Peace Learning Center, a pistol and archery range, retreat centers and a full 36-hole golf course. Seasonal activities include cross–country skiing, swimming, sailing, canoeing, and fishing.

EAGLE HIGHLANDS PARK
Indy NW

4201 Eagle Creek Pkwy.
Indianapolis, IN 46254
(317) 327-7036

This park has a great play structure and swings; WonderDad can push his kids as high as the sky.

MIDWEST SPORTS COMPLEX INC.
Indy NW

7509 New Augusta Rd.
Indianapolis, IN 46268
(317) 875-8833

WonderDad will find a variety of indoor and outdoor activities to do at this complex.

NORTHWESTWAY PARK
Indy NW

5253 W 62nd St.
Indianapolis, IN 46268
(317) 327-7341

WonderDad and his kids can spend time here on the playground, in the pool, or playing disc golf.

83

WISH PARK
Indy NW

2602 Westlane Rd.
Indianapolis, IN 46268
(317) 327-7036

This has a great play structure and is also a Supervised Play Site, which means it hosts a free summer day camp!

CARSON PARK
Indy W

5400 S High School Rd.
Indianapolis, IN 46221
(317) 888-0070

The park is very simple and is great for WonderDads and kids to bring their lunch to and enjoy. The park has a playground, picnic areas, a walking trail, and is filled with a lot of grassy areas to romp around.

CHAPEL HILL PARK
Indy W

900 Girls School Rd.
Indianapolis, IN 46214
(317) 327-7036

Chapel Hill Park sits on 6.39 acres of land directly south of Chapel Hill Church. The park plays hosts to softball games and various special events. Dads and kids can enjoy playing on the playground and watching softball games being played by local leagues.

CHRISTINA OAKS PARK
Indy W

4205 W Washington St.
Indianapolis, IN 46241
(317) 327-7036

WonderDads and kids can get plenty of exercise running from the playground to the two basketball courts. The park also has swing sets, a play structure, and some grassy areas to sit down on and watch the kids play all day.

KRANNERT AQUATIC CENTER
Indy W

605 S High School Rd.
Indianapolis, IN 46241
(317) 327-7334

This park offers the best of both worlds. Inside and outside fun for WonderDads and kids. The indoor pool is open all year, so come on in and make a splash with the kids. The park also has an outdoor pool, fitness trails, a fishing pond, softball diamonds, football field, and tennis courts.

OUTDOOR PARKS

SOUTHWESTWAY PARK

Indy W

8400 Mann Rd.
Indianapolis, IN 46221
(317) 327-7379

Southwestway Park is joined with Winding River golf course and Cottonwood Lakes, so WonderDads and kids can enjoy all three places at once. There is a baseball field, shelters, a concession stand, soccer fields, hiking trails, and a great playground. In the park there is Mann Hill, which is the highest bluff, rising more than 150 feet above the surrounding land. It's perfect for sledding in the winter.

BLUFF PARK

Southport

555 W Hanna Ave.
Indianapolis, IN 46217
(317) 327-7806

The park is home to organized softball, soccer, and rugby leagues. WonderDads and the kids can watch a game in progress or practice some kicking with their own soccer ball.

GUSTAFSON PARK

Southport

3110 Moller Rd.
Indianapolis, IN 46227
(317) 327-7334

Kids can play on the playground after they swim in the outdoor pool at this park. WonderDad will enjoy the day with his kids on a hot sunny day at this park.

MIKE'S SOUTHPORT FISHING LAKES

Southport

4141 W Southport Rd.
Indianapolis, IN 46217
(317) 888-9083

If you are in the mood to show your kid how to fish, then this is a great location for you. Bring your own bait or buy some at the nearby bait store and get ready to rock and roll.

PERRY PARK

Southport

451 E Stop 11 Rd.
Indianapolis, IN 46227
(317) 889-0825

This park has a lot of activities for WonderDads and kids to do together. The park has an indoor ice and in–line skating rink, tennis courts, a super playground, an outdoor basketball court, and an aquatic center with play equipment and two waterslides.

TOLIN-AKEMAN PARK   Southport

4459 Shelbyville Rd.
Indianapolis, IN 46237
(317) 327-7806

This park has a big play structure for the kids to climb up and down on.
There are also some swing sets for the kids to work on pumping their legs
to see how high they can swing without WonderDad pushing them. This
is a nice park to go to after nap time or after school is over for the day.
WonderDad and his kids can burn off some energy before going home
for dinner.

THE BEST DAD/CHILD
SPORTING EVENTS

CONSECO FIELDHOUSE
Downtown

125 S Pennsylvania St.
Indianapolis, IN 46204
(317) 917-2755

Basketball home of the NBA Indianapolis Paces and WNBA Indiana Fever. Both male and female basketball teams are great for WonderDad to bring his kids to see. Pacers play from October to April and the Fevers play from May to August.

INDIANAPOLIS MOTOR SPEEDWAY
Downtown

4790 W 16th St.
Indianapolis, IN 46222
(317) 484-6784 | www.indianapolismotorspeedway.com

May is crazy in Indianapolis, so WonderDad may want to call ahead to see what events are taking place. Indianapolis is known as the racing capital of the world and the season runs from May to September. The special events are The Indianapolis 500, Allstate 400 at the Brickyard, NASCA Spirit Cup Series, and Red Bull Indy GP motorcycle racing.

INDIANA UNIVERSITY NATATORIUM
Downtown

901 W New York St.
Indianapolis, IN 46202
(317) 274-3518

IHSAA Boys and Girls swimming championships and USA Olympic Swimming occur here. Diving and synchronized swim trials also take place here. WonderDads with swimmers will want to bring his kids when swim trials are announced.

LUCAS OIL STADIUM
Downtown

500 S Capitol Ave.
Indianapolis, IN 46225
(317) 262- 8600 | www.lucasoilstadium.com

This is the place to see the famous Indianapolis Colts, and quarterback Peyton Manning play NFL football. The Colts play from August to January. Tickets are tough to come by, so if you think your kids would love to take in an NFL game, start planning early.

MAJOR TAYLOR VELODROME AND LAKE SULLIVAN BMX TRACK
Downtown

349 Cold Spring Rd.
Indianapolis, IN 46228
(317) 327-8356

Hosts national biking competitions. Lake Sullivan BMX Track (closed for winter), Major Taylor Velodrome (closed for winter), and Major Taylor Skate Park are FREE and open every day. WonderDad and his kids can come and skateboard or wait for dates on biking competitions.

VICTORY FIELD HOUSE
Downtown

501 W Maryland St.
Indianapolis, IN 46225
(317) 269-3545 | www.indyindians.com

This is the home of AAA minor league baseball's Indianapolis Indians. They play from April to September. WonderDads and kids should come at least once to this field house, as every seat is a good seat to see the game.

WILBUR H. SHAW SOAP BOX DERBY RACE TRACK
Downtown

3001 Cold Spring Rd.
Indianapolis, IN 46228
(317) 327-7037

This is the longest Soap Box Derby Track in the country, measuring 1000 feet. All Soap Box Derby racing in Indianapolis is sanctioned by either the All-American Soap Box Derby or National Derby Rallies. Racing is open to those from 8 through 20 years of age in National Derby Rallies racing and from 9 through 16 in All-American racing.

NAPTOWN ROLLER GIRLS
Indy E

973 N Shadeland PMB#168
Indianapolis, IN 46219
(317) 522-1958 | www.naptownrollergirls.com

This is a fabulous team that WonderDad should bring his kids to see. Call or visit the website to get more information. NRG is a member of the Women's Flat-Track Derby Association, which is a national governing body for women's amateur flat-track roller derby in the U.S.

O'REILLY RACEWAY PARK

Indy E

10267 E US Highway 136
Indianapolis, IN 46234
(317) 291-4090

NHRA Drag Racing, MAC Tools U.S. Nationals, United States Auto Club Racing, and ARCA Racing Series take place here. WonderDads will find a host of different racing teams to enjoy with his kids.

BUTLER BULLDOGS
BUTLER UNIVERSITY

Indy N

4600 Sunset Ave.
Indianapolis, IN 46208
(800) 368-6852 | www.butlersports.com

The Bulldogs have made appearances in NCAA National Championship Tournaments in men's and women's basketball, men's soccer, volleyball, men's cross country, lacrosse, and baseball. Visit the website for games and ticket prices. The Bulldogs are great to see in person, so WonderDad should try to get tickets when they are playing at home.

INDIANA SPEED

Indy N

Park Tudor School, 7200 N College Ave.
Indianapolis, IN 46250
www.indianaspeed.com

Indiana Speed Women's Football LLC is Indiana's only professional Women's football team. Their playing season runs April through July and games are on Saturday evenings at 7pm at Park Tudor. For more information and tickets, visit the website. This is a great chance to show kids that football can be played by both men and women.

PEPSI COLISEUM

Indy N

1202 E 38th St.
Indianapolis, IN 46205
(317) 927-7622

United States Hockey League team the Indiana Ice play here from October to March every year.

THE BEST DAD/CHILD
UNIQUE ADVENTURES

AMISH ACRES HISTORIC FARM & HERITAGE RESORT

1600 W Market St.
Nappanee, IN 46550
(800) 800-4942

Travel time from Indianapolis is 2 hours and 45 minutes. The Amish live a life that is much simpler than most people. WonderDad and his kids will enjoy touring the Amish Acres and have 2 great packages to choose from: 1. Day Trippers – $28.95 adult, $11.95 child, includes House & Farm Tour, Farm Wagon Ride, Tour Documentary Films; Genesis, Exodus, and Bonnets and Britches, Award Winning Family Style Thresher's Dinner, and Shopping Coupons (Worth $55 in savings). The other day trip package is more expensive, but gives you a lot more time to spend on Amish Acres meeting people and enjoying the culture. 2. Bonnets & Britches Package – Day Trippers $54.85 adult, $43.85 student (12-17), $19.85 child (4-12), and includes House & Farm Tour, Farm Wagon Ride Tour, Documentary Films; Genesis and Exodus of the Amish, and Bonnets and Britches, Award Winning Family Style Thresher's Dinner, Plain and Fancy musical in the Round Barn Theatre (or any of the six additional live performances), Second Show Theatre Discount of $6 off single adult ticket, and Valuable Shopping Coupons (Worth $55 in savings). Call in advance to get details on when live performances take place and to make reservations.

ATLANTIS WATER PARK

515 Marriott Dr.
Clarksville, IN 47129
(812) 285-0863

Travel time from Indianapolis is 2 hours. Admission is $8 per person on weekdays and $10 per person on weekends and holidays. Atlantis Water Park features Tsunami Sea, a large exhilarating wave pool, Mount Olympus, a 43' towering maze of water slides, and King Neptune's Cove, a perfectly sized water space for the smaller water tikes.

BLUESPRING CAVERNS

1459 Bluespring Cavern Rd.
Bedford, IN 47421
(812) 279-947 | www.bluespringcaverns.com

Travel time from Indianapolis is 1 hour and 30 minutes. Open Memorial Day to Labor Day everyday from 9am-5pm. Call to make reservations, as they do not take admission on site. Tickets for the tour are $14 for adults and $7 for Children ages 3 through 15. The tour is not recommended for infants and very young children. The walk into the Caverns to the tour boats and back to the surface is 800-feet and is a fairly steep ramp. This is an adventure that will be unforgettable as WonderDad and the kids journey into the cavern. This is a wonderful tour of the caverns from below riding in a boat. WonderDad and kids can see blind crayfish living in the water. The trip is 1¼ miles long and can be dark and cold, so dressing in extra layers is advised.

CARTER'S ANTIQUE TOY MUSEUM

91 S Main St.

Zionsville, IN 46077

(317) 733-1650 | www.carterstoymuseum.com

Travel time from Indianapolis is 30 minutes. Open April to December and hours are Tuesday-Saturday, 11am to 5pm. Admission: $5 for adults, $3 for children. Kids get free rides with admission. Games and toys for both WonderDad and his own kids to enjoy. There are 3 stories of antique toys, coin–op rides and real bumper cars that can all be ridden. Approximately 50,000 toys to remember your childhood, with antiques from 1890-1970! Dad will surely find his way to the antique arcade games from yesteryear. After all the fun, visit the Old Tyme Soda Shop with food and ice cream.

CIRCUS CITY FESTIVAL, INC.

154 N Broadway

Peru, IN 46970

(765) 472-3918

Travel time from Indianapolis is 1 hour and 30 minutes. This popular museum, located in the Circus City Center, is filled with photos, miniatures, displays, and costumes from circus past. The museum is open Monday-Friday. During Circus Week enjoy the many circus wagons displayed outside the museum as well as extended hours before and after each circus performance. Join in the celebration of Peru's Circus Heritage for 9 days in July.

CROWN PLAZA AT HISTORIC UNION STATION

123 W Louisiana St.

Indianapolis, IN 46225

(317) 631-2221

Located in downtown Indianapolis this is a sleepover party for Wonder-Dad and his kids. It costs $179 a night to stay in an authentic Pullman train car room. The rooms are small with 2 beds, but are decorated as they once were. If you and your kids love trains and want to have an adventure to treasure, then spending the night at this downtown hotel is worth the splurge.

UNIQUE ADVENTURES

FAIR OAKS FARMS

856 N 600 E
Fair Oaks, IN 47943
(877) 536-1194

Travel time from Indianapolis is 2 hours. Adults $10, Children 3-12 $7. Learn more about farming and cows by visiting this huge farm. Take a tour and see cheese and ice cream being made in the Dairy Processing plant. If you visit after Memorial Day, you'll be able to go to "Mooville", a section devoted to younger children. Catch some major air on the gigantic Dairy Air jumping pillow. The kids can hang tight as they rock climb to Udder Heights on a 25-foot milk bottle. The kids will love the String Cheese Maze. The little ones can even enjoy a ride on the Moo Choo train or race around the track on the green Holstein Haulers.

HOLIDAY WORLD AND SPLASH'N SAFARI

452 E Christmas Blvd.
Santa Claus, IN 47579
(877) GO-FAMILY | www.holidayworld.com

Travel time from Indianapolis is 3 hours. General Admission is $42.95 for one day and $64.95 for 2 days. Guests under –54"/Senior 60+ are $32.95 for one day and $54.95 for 2 days. Children 2 and under are free. This is a 3 hour drive south from Indianapolis, so staying overnight and seeing everything on the weekend would be a good idea. This amusement park is a must for fans of rides and of Santa Claus. The park is very clean and the rides have a great history of success throughout the years. They offer free refills, so the kids and dad will get hyped up on soft drinks. Mr. and Mrs. Claus make many appearances, especially in the section for smaller kids. While the park is wonderful, dad should also visit the Santa Claus Museum while in town. If the kids have their christmas lists filled out in the summer, mail them from here to be post-marked Santa Claus!

HUNTER'S HONEY FARM

3440 Hancock Ridge Rd.
Martinsville, IN 46151
(765) 537-9430 | www.HuntersHoneyFarm.com

Travel time from Indianapolis is 30 minutes. Open Monday-Saturday 9am-6pm and Sundays from 12pm-6pm. $4.50 per person, kids under 2 are free. If your kids love honey then this is the place for WonderDad to buzz over for an adventure. Locally owned and operated for over 90 years. Take a tour and learn how honey is made, watch it get extracted and bottled, learn about how candles are made and explore the grounds. Candle Rolling to make your own candle is $2.50 per candle.

INDIANA DUNES NATIONAL LAKESHORE

1100 N Mineral Springs Rd.
Porter, IN 46304
(866) 622-6746 or (219) 926-7561

Travel time from Indianapolis is 2 hours and 45 minutes. Admission into the park is $4-$10. Kids can go to the only lifeguarded beach area from mid-May through Labor Day. West Beach, the most heavily used beach, features a bath house with showers, picnic area, hiking trails, concessions, interpretive displays, and is the favorite for dads. The sand dunes WonderDad and his kids will discover will make it hard for even a super hero to climb up and down.

INDIANA TRANSPORTATION MUSEUM

Forest Park , 701 Cicero Rd.
Noblesville, IN 46060
(317) 524-1585

Travel time from Indianapolis is 45 minutes. The Indiana Transportation Museum is only open on weekends and is great fun for train lovers of all ages. Stay the whole day after visiting the museum at Forest Park and enjoy five picnic shelters, two playgrounds, horseshoe pits, volleyball courts, basketball courts, a running carousel, Tom Thumb putt-putt course, and swimming at the aquatic center. Dads and kids can jump aboard the Pizza Train to Tipton for dinner. The train travels from Noblesville and goes all the way through Hamilton County's northside until it stops in Tipton County at Tipton's Train Station.

KOKOMO BEACH FAMILY AQUATIC CENTER

804 W Park Ave.
Kokomo, IN 46901
(765) 456-7540

Travel time from Indianapolis is 1 hour and 15 minutes. Open from Memorial Day to Labor Day. Adults are $6 and Children are $5. WonderDad and his kids will find several water park attractions, like a waterslide, kids' slide, and lazy river. There is also a leisure pool and competition & lap pool for your enjoyment. This is a great place to relax and enjoy the summer. The kids who have visited here come back many more times through the summer.

MARENGO CAVE

400 E State Rd. 64
Marengo, IN 47140
(888) 702-2837 | www.marengocave.com

Travel time from Indianapolis is 2 hours and 30 minutes. The Crystal Palace Tour is 40 minutes and great for dads with small kids. Prices for this tour: children 3 and younger are free, $7 child, and $13.50 for adults. The caves and taverns are a beautiful sight to see. Gemstone mining for Wonder-Dad's kids will be an adventure on its own. Prices vary from $5.99 to $8.99 for gems, fossils, and arrowheads. Prices include: mining materials, plastic bag for gems, and gem identification card.

MUNCIE CHILDREN'S MUSEUM

515 S High St.
Muncie, IN 47305
(765) 286-1660 | www.munciechildrensmuseum.com

Travel time from Indianapolis is 1 hour. Admission is $6 for ages 1-100, closed on Mondays. The exhibits WonderDad will surely not want to miss are the "Tot Spot" for kids under 2, "Outdoor Learning Center" with a tree house and a performance area, and "The Senses," a hands-on exhibit with a larger-than-life brain, ear, eye, hand, mouth, and nose. Wonder-Dad will be nostalgic visiting the famous Garfield Exhibit. WonderDad and his kids can see the evolution of Garfield from beginning to now. Learn how to draw Garfield and discover the secrets of Garfield's creation.

STUDEBAKER NATIONAL MUSEUM

201 S Chapin St.
South Bend, IN 46601
(800) 391-5600 | www.studebakermuseum.org

Travel time from Indianapolis is 3 hours. Open Monday-Saturday from 10am-5pm and Sundays from 12pm-5pm. Admission is free for kids 5 and younger, $5 for students over 6, and $8 for adults. This is a must see museum for anyone who loves old cars. Vehicles stored here are placed in "visible storage" on the ground floor, with units rotated off the ramps for display on the three floors of the museum. The main floor has the carriage Abraham Lincoln rode to Ford's Theater on the night he was assassinated. Also among the three floors are military trucks and vehicles, which are sure to fascinate WonderDad's kids.

TRADERS POINT CREAMERY

9101 Moore Rd.
Zionsville, IN 46077
(317) 733-1700

Travel time from Indianapolis is 30 minutes. Call for current prices and hours they are open. Self–Guided Tour: These family friendly tours are available everyday from 9am–5pm. Visit the calves and chickens, walk out to the pasture to see the herd, visit the milking parlor, and watch production while looking through the Creamery window. If possible, call some other WonderDads up and book a private tour of the farm for a real treat. The kids won't mind being at the farm longer if they get to taste samples! Option to choose if you have at least 10 people reserved is the "Private Tour, Tasting & Ice Cream." After the private tour, you will be served samples of yogurts, cheese, and chocolate milk, and a full serving of ice cream. This irresistible package can be added for an extra $6 per person. Dads should plan on staying an extra 45 minutes for the tasting and ice cream. Or for a seasonal delight of tours you can do the "Hand Milking & Hot Chocolate Tour" (December through February Only). This private tour includes the history of the farm, learning about the life–cycle of cows, the interdependent relationship of livestock and humans, and a brief discussion about processing methods. The highlight of this tour, of course, is the opportunity to hand–milk one of the gentle and patient cows! The tour culminates with a cup of Traders Point Creamery's smooth and delicious Hot Chocolate Milk. This tour will last approximately 1 hour. Hand Milking group sizes: Minimum 10 people/Maximum 30 people.

TROPICANOE COVE

1915 Scott St.
Lafayette, IN 47904
(765) 807-1531

Travel time from Indianapolis is 1 hour. Open Memorial Day Weekend to Labor Day Weekend, Wednesdays 11am - 8pm (Family Night). Costs vary by child's height, but daily admission is $6 or less per person. WonderDad and kids will love this facility with pool, lazy river, body, and tube slides. With a 299 foot Banana Peel tube slide and 640 foot lazy river, WonderDad can be adventurous or just relax. Frog Pond offers zero depth entry and 168,000 galloons of crystal clear water. Sunfish Bay is a water playground.

TURKEY RUN STATE PARK

8121 E Park Rd.
Marshall, IN 47859
(765) 597-2635

Travel time from Indianapolis is 1 hour and 30 minutes. $4 Gate fee (Monday–Thursday), $5 Gate fee (Friday-Sunday, Holidays) for noncommercial vehicles which have INDIANA license plates. This is a beautiful state park with various trails to walk along. There is a playground in the front area near where all the different trails start. WonderDad's kids will love finding the correct signs of the trail they are following as they are marked. The signs will tell you how long each trail is as you walk along the waters, over bridges, near little caves, and in some spots that are picture perfect. There are special areas for canoeing, swimming, and fishing. There is also a planetarium for WonderDads and kids to look at the stars in the evening.

WOLF PARK

4004 E 800 N
Battle Ground, IN 47920
(765) 567-2265 | www.wolfpark.org

Travel time from Indianapolis is 1 hour and 15 minutes. Guided tours are open May through November from 1pm-5pm on Tuesdays-Fridays. Tour prices are children under 5 free, children 6-13 are $5, and 14 and older are $7. Surprise your kids by visiting a park devoted to wolves. The Wolf Park wolves interact with humans by being socialized when they are only 2 weeks old. The kids will learn new information by watching the wolves and taking the tour of the park. A popular highlight of this park is "Howl Nights" which are held on Fridays and Saturdays at 7:30pm. Howl Nights: demonstration, lecture, and howling with wolves. Prices are free for children under 5, $5 for children 6-13, and $7 for anyone 14 and older. In the early evening when the wolves are most active, the members of the audience are encouraged to howl and then the wolves join in.

YOGI BEAR'S CAMP RESORT AT BARTON LAKE, INC.

140 Ln. 201 Barton Lake
Fremont, IN 46737

For Reservations: (800) 375-6063 For Information: (260) 833-1114

Travel time from Indianapolis is 3 hours. This park has everything a dad and his kids could want for either a one night stay or a long weekend away. With camp sites, cabins, and deluxe cottages, this park can accommodate all of your camping needs! Facilities include an indoor pool, thee outdoor pools, a water splash park, three giant water slides, paddle boat & row boat rentals, five playgrounds, laundry facilities, fully-stocked camping store, snack bar, game room, mini-golf, swimming beach, Water Wars, Pedal Cart rental, golf cart rental, a large recreation building, kiddy train rides, wagon rides, lighted basketball courts, horseshoes, sand volleyball courts, wagon/stroller rental, Free Wi-Fi, showers and restrooms. Not to mention Yogi Bear™ and his friends Boo Boo™, Cindy Bear™ and Ranger Smith™!

UNIQUE ADVENTURES

ABOUT THE AUTHOR

Angela Arlington lives north of Indianapolis in Westfield with her 12 year old son Aaron and her dog Cassie. She is a developmental therapist and works with kids 3 and under with developmental delays. Her passions include reading, writing, autism, and advocating for early intervention and education for all children. This is her first published book.

THANK YOUS

Miss Arlington would like to express her gratitude for all the great ideas and encouragement she received from the following people: Jason Bright, Monica Holloway, Debbie Myers, Chris Maples, Kurt and Susan Pieples, and Ken Steppe.

Breinigsville, PA USA
13 March 2011
257570BV00004B/2/P